*2ⁿᵈ Edition*

# THE SHYNESS & SOCIAL ANXIETY SYSTEM MANUAL

SEAN COOPER

**LIMIT OF LIABILITY AND DISCLAIMER:**

This manual is based on personal experience and is designed to provide information about the subject matter covered. Every effort has been made to make it as complete and accurate as possible. All information provided through this text and associated audio program and websites are for informational purposes only and are not intended to replace the care, advice, or instruction of a medical professional. Its author, or company, will not be held liable in any way for the information contained through the website or this text. Users should consult a physician before making any lifestyle, dietary, or other health or psychologically related changes. This book solely represents its author's opinion. You are responsible for your own behavior, and none of this book is to be considered personal, psychological, or medical advice. See a Doctor before making any changes whatsoever to your lifestyle (including both psychological and physiological changes). Results will vary for individual users.

The author shall have neither liability nor responsibility to any person or entity with respect to any loss or damage caused or alleged to be caused directly or indirectly by the information covered in this manual.

**TRADEMARKS:**

Any trademarks, service marks, product names or named features are assumed to be the property of their respective owners, and are used for reference only.

**SHARING THIS DOCUMENT:**

It's often said that, "Information wants to be free!" I absolutely, positively enjoy writing. And I wish I could give away everything I write - but I can't. I've chosen to self-publish my work. This is my only 9-to-5. It's how I make my living... how I put food on the table and pay my rent. I ask that you please respect the work I do by not giving away or reselling this guide. I sincerely thank you for that respect!

*To Your Success,*
*Sean Cooper*

ISBN-10: 1482504448

ISBN-13: 978-1482504446

# Wait! Before You Continue Claim Your FREE Gifts!

Hey, Sean Cooper here.

As a special "Thank You" for buying my book, I'm going to give you these <u>3 free gifts</u> as a surprise bonus:

1. **"How To Always Know What To Say Next" Report** – This report will show you a simple trick to never run out of things to say again. *(Imagine never needing to worry about creating awkward silences or getting a "blank mind"!)*
2. **"Social Circle From Scratch" Report** – This 43 page report will teach you the things you may not have learned while growing up about making friends and getting people to see you as an interesting person.
3. **Weekly email tips and advice** – I'll email you my latest, most cutting-edge techniques and insights into overcoming shyness and social anxiety. *(I promise not to spam you, and you'll be able to unsubscribe from this newsletter any time you want.)*

## To Claim Your Free Gifts, Go Here Now:
### www.ShynessSocialAnxiety.com/freegift/

# CONTENTS

# Part 1

# How To "Rewire" Your Brain To Overcome Shyness Or Cure Social Anxiety

# Chapter 1
# Introduction: Who I Am And How To Use This Manual

**Hey, my name is Sean** and the first thing you should know about me is I am not a psychologist, psychiatrist, or therapist.

I'm not an expert on psychology, either. I don't have a PhD, or a degree in psychology or a degree in anything else for that matter. In fact, the only thing I consider myself an "expert" about is

I think I know how almost anyone who has shyness or social anxiety can overcome their loneliness, nervousness and quietness .. using the right strategy!

I know because *I* did it.

I'd like to start off by telling you a little bit about me and how this system came into existence.

# What's My Story?

I used to have very bad social anxiety. How bad was it? Let me give you some examples ...

- **I couldn't talk to people without feeling nervous.**
- I was completely **unable to hold a regular conversation** with someone.
- **I couldn't even hold eye contact** with anyone most of the time.
- And so, as a result, all throughout my school years **I had basically no friends or social life.**

- To add on top of this, **my self esteem was non-existent**. Although I was at the top of almost every class when it came to marks, and I had many talents and abilities that I could be proud of, my opinion of myself was very low.

- **I even had extreme insecurities about my physical appearance.** I thought I looked terrible, I was so insecure about my teeth that I was even afraid to smile.

- **I was afraid to express myself or to be happy.** I was never loud or outgoing because when people put their attention on me, I immediately felt very anxious and afraid.

- **If I was in a social situation, I felt anxiety constantly.** I felt stress and worry constantly. I really had no idea what was wrong with me growing up. People told me that I was shy and quiet, and so I began to accept that this is just the way I am.

That is my background. That is the situation which I came from.

Why am I telling you all this? To show you that personal transformation really is possible, no matter how hopeless you think you are.

Everything I write or speak about overcoming shyness or social anxiety is very carefully constructed so that you can change yourself in the shortest time possible. I've researched through almost all of the books, self help programs, and therapy options out there and kept only the information that actually helps.

**But I had to throw most of what I read right into the garbage can.** Most of the advice written in this area is based either in common sense or academic theory. So it's either something everyone already knows (like telling you to have a good posture) or it's advice that you can't apply in your daily life because it's too abstract.

See, a lot of people who write about overcoming shyness or social anxiety are only able to study it academically from the outside. But, because they have never undergone the actual process of overcoming it themselves or coached anyone else, they can't give you the necessary inner mindset shifts required. My system aims to change all that.

# A Manual For Personal Change

If you are struggling to overcome shyness or social anxiety, then **I hope this book is your wake up call.** In here I'll share with you the exact same strategies and techniques that I and countless others have used to overcome our shyness and social anxiety and, in doing so, changed our lives.

You're about to be introduced to knowledge and information that can have such an amazing impact on your life.

If you read this book and make an ongoing effort to learn its contents, then your way of interacting with other people can change. You can change your core personality from someone who is anxious and withdrawn, to someone who is generally relaxed and at ease in most social situations.

# I'll Tell You Exactly What To Do and When

Best of all, you'll learn the truth about overcoming shyness and social anxiety without having to go through as much of the painful failure and embarrassment that other people have suffered.

Psychologists, therapists and self help writers tend to focus on telling shy people that they should "get out more" and get more experience (which is great), but they never tell you exactly what you should do while in these situations. The truth is, you need specific, concrete directions so you can avoid embarrassment and grow.

**It's taken me a long time to figure out the things you're about to learn.** I've spent literally years on this stuff and discovered that there's a few core principles for overcoming shyness or social anxiety that work. These principles work amazingly.

If you follow the principles and make the necessary changes I have laid out in this book, you will begin overcoming your shyness or social anxiety 10x faster than if you tried to do it all on your own. In fact, trying to overcome shyness or social anxiety on your own without making the changes in thinking and behavior I outline in this book is next to impossible. You'll just continue reinforcing the same bad habits and making the same mistakes.

# How To Use This System

**This system is jam-packed with information.** It's meant to be used as a reference. The best way to use it is to read and find all the parts you like and all of the ideas, skills, and techniques upon which you would like to improve. Then take those sections and write them down or print them out so you can remind yourself. Read them out loud and maybe talk about it with other shy people you know who might need the help of this book.

**But don't assume that reading it once will solve all your problems.** Make a note when you find a section that applies to your situation. Get a journal and jot down the ideas that grab your attention. Keep these ideas processing in your mind.

The best thing to do is to take one piece of advice and apply it immediately. Let it set for maybe a week, and then continue, applying another.

# It's Not Enough to Know All the Info You Must Go and Apply It

Right now it's up to you. I can't do all the learning and practice for you. It's you who has got to make the decision that you'll do whatever it takes to get to that next level of understanding.

Learning social and conversational skills is a lot like learning to play a musical instrument. **It takes practice and repetition.** At first none of it makes any sense. Sometimes it seems as though all of your practice isn't making a difference. But if you keep at it, eventually you'll be playing songs. And then you'll be writing songs. The next thing you know, you've become a master.

Let me put it to you another way

**Imagine you went into the gym and hired a personal trainer.** They taught you everything there was to know about fitness. But then you never worked out and ate junk food all day.

If you do not apply what you learn in this book, then the information by itself is useless to you. But if you put in the work, you can experience a complete transformation.

**This is not a magic pill.** You need experience out in the real world. If you never had a social life throughout high school, that means that now is the time to get out there and get that social experience you're missing.

# You Need a Long-Term Level Of Commitment

Like learning any new skill, there are going to be ups and downs. You'll make brief spurts of progress, then decline to a level slightly higher than the one you were at before. Your progress may look something like this:

In order to master social skills and permanently destroy your shyness or social anxiety, it takes persistence. **You have to be willing to practice diligently, striving to hone your skills even when it seems like you are getting nowhere in your progress or even going backwards.**

In the long-term, your success will become evident. So don't give up just because you experience short-term setbacks and disappointments.

So take this book and use it as a workbook. Come back to it often. Reread the parts that you want to learn and integrate them in your daily life. Take a look and learn from some of the other books and information I've referenced. And most importantly, DON'T STOP READING UNTIL YOU'RE DOING IT.

Many people make the mistake of reading a book and say "I know that stuff" before they've mastered the information. Don't make this mistake yourself. Keep reading and practicing until you HAVE IT DOWN.

Most people who have shyness or social anxiety don't make progress because they don't take action. They are dabblers who don't have the ability or willpower to stick at anything they want to accomplish in their life. I'm not going to lie to you or BS you. Everything I tell you is going to be the honest truth as far as I know it.

**There's lots of people out there who will tell you what you want to hear.** They'll try to tell you that you can hypnotize yourself into being confident, or rely on pills to avoid anxiety, or something else equally ridiculous. The difference with me is that I don't care if what I say makes you uncomfortable.

It SHOULD make you uncomfortable. What we are trying to accomplish here is something not ordinary, but very extraordinary. If you want to change who you are at a deep, core level, then you should get used to being uncomfortable.

Most people never change because they like to stick in their comfort zone. Their fear of the unknown makes them stay the same their whole life. If you want to become different, you'll have to take a different approach.

However, if you do choose to apply it, then the amount of change you experience will shock you. You will be shocked at how much different you will be able to act and how much differently people will start treating you.

So let's get to the point.

# What Exactly Do I Teach, And Why Is It So Effective?

I teach a very specific set of principles that are designed to change the way you think and the way you behave. If you want to overcome social anxiety, then these are the only two areas you need to work on: your thoughts, and your behavior.

If you have taken a look through my system, then you would have noticed that I have split it up into three parts:

- **Part 1: How To "Rewire" Your Brain To Overcome Shyness Or Cure Social Anxiety**
- **Part 2: Proven Anxiety Reducing Techniques**
- **Part 3: Changing How You Think**

The first two parts deal with changing your behavior, and part three deals with changing your thinking. Think about this like upgrading a computer. Changing your outer behavior is like upgrading the hardware. Changing your inner thoughts and beliefs is like upgrading the software.

Although changing your behavior is very important, you cannot overcome shyness or social anxiety through behavior change alone. You must attack the problem deeper.

**Shyness and social anxiety are caused by bad patterns of thinking.** If you didn't think the way you do now, then you wouldn't have your problems. This is why the third part of this system is, in my opinion, the most important one. It's in the third part that you'll probably be getting a lot of "aha" moments and deep insights into how to overcome your shyness or social anxiety.

# How Much Is This All Really Worth?

Now, if you stop and consider just how much effort and research I put into the content of the system, it's easy to see how it's a bargain.

**If you want to go and talk to a therapist, then they will usually charge you at least $150 an hour.** And to see any lasting effects, you'll have to go at least once a week. So, unless you have about $600 a month to spend on a high quality, professional therapist, then it's going to be hard to access the same type of information that I will share with you here.

In fact, even professional therapists who charge up to $600 a month have little experience of what it is like to actually have social anxiety. The best they can do is repeat some technique or information they learned and hope it will work for you. If they've never had to deal with social anxiety themselves, there's only so much they can offer to others.

Of course, I have nothing against therapists. I know many definitely help out a lot of people, and if you go see one they may help you resolve a lot of your own emotional issues as well. The only point I'm trying to make is that a therapist may not be a realistic solution for everyone. For some people it's too expensive, for others it's not effective.

# Learn At Your Own Pace From The Comfort Of Your Home

And some people who have very extreme social anxiety will never even think of going to see a therapist because their anxiety at the moment is too great. They are way too afraid of the idea of admitting they need help for their shyness or social anxiety to even think of seeing a therapist at this point in their life.

This is why it's really a pleasure for me to be able to reach so many people through the internet that otherwise would be lost and without a direction. Even if you are the most antisocial person in the world, you can still reach the information and what I teach through the internet and learn how to take the first steps in improving your life.

This is an amazing opportunity that technology has opened up in recent years that was not there before. Now you can learn from the comfort of your own home, at a very low cost, and make improvements in your own life.

Whatever you have come here to accomplish, I want to help you get there. If you want a few friends or to overcome your shyness around the opposite sex, my information will help you move in the right direction. I try to make it very practical and applicable, and just share with you my own experiences learning everything about this issue and then turning around and teaching it to others. The things which I have found to make a real difference in my own life, as well as in the lives of my students.

# Send Me Your Feedback

**I get emails all the time from people all around the world telling me that the information I teach is curing their shyness or social anxiety.** Once in a while, I get a professional therapist or social skills coach emailing me to say the method I teach is the best combination of tools out there.

In fact, I posted a couple of these emails on my website.

One, from a Licensed Clinical Psychologist living near Chicago called Dr. Todd Snyder. He specializes in the areas of social anxiety and relationships and has actually battled social anxiety himself.

Here's what he had to say about my system and membership website:

> "As a clinical psychologist specializing in social anxiety and self-help systems, I was amazed at how well Sean has distilled many of the principles that can actually make a difference for those of us who battle social anxiety. Sean's information is straight to the point and focused on some of the most critical skills for managing shyness and anxiety."
>
> **- Dr. Todd Snyder**

Another email came in from a professional communication coach specializing in social success named Eduard Ezeanu. He has a B.A. in Psychology and he has been coaching people in communication skills and confidence for the past 9 years. Here's what he said after he read my system:

> "As a former shy, "invisible" guy myself, I find something fascinating in what Sean teaches in this system because you can tell he's been through it, he knows personally what it's like to have shyness and social anxiety, and he grasped how to beat it.
>
> The Shyness and Social Anxiety System got me realizing things I wasn't aware of about overcoming shyness. This is probably the finest proof I can give of the quality of this system, considering that I coach shy people almost on a daily basis and I believe I know a thing or two about overcoming shyness. If you struggle with shyness or social anxiety, coaching is out of your financial range and you're looking for a quality information product to help you make real progress, this system is it."
>
> **-Eduard Ezeanu**

These are just two out of many emails I receive, proving to me without a shadow of a doubt that overcoming shyness and social anxiety is possible with the right tools. It's not a personality trait, it's not something you are born with. It's just a set of old habits of thinking and behavior that you can erase with the right tools.

There's so many people out there who miss out on that interpersonal dimension of life because of their social anxiety. This is a shame, because they may actually be great people on the inside, but their fear holds them back from being confident when they want to be and having the types of social circle and relationships that most people take for granted.

Remember, I'm not trying to teach you how to become superhuman here. You don't have to become a super confident, extroverted social butterfly to make this work. **Really, the goal is to just have a very normal, natural, healthy level of social relationships in your life.** To be able to express yourself comfortably, confidently and effectively in social situations. To stop feeling, anxious, insecure, nervous and tense around people.

**And I truly believe anyone can accomplish this if they choose to work at it.** Anyone can reach the very modest goal of feeling okay and adequate with who you are, and feeling like other people will accept you for who you are. This is the very core of what I teach, and I hope you stick around.

Congratulations, by the way. You're taking an amazing step by investing in your own life to figure things out. If you stay with it, you'll have amazing results in lots of other areas.

Do me a favor. E-mail me with your ideas, comments, and complaints. I want to know what you think. You can email me at:

**sean@shynesssocialanxiety.com**

# Chapter 2
# What Is Shyness And Social Anxiety?

**Once you have "woken up" and decided to fix your shyness or social anxiety, the next step is to figure out exactly what it is.**

Believe it or not, most people who have shyness or social anxiety actually don't have much of an idea of what their condition is, how it works, or where it came from. This chapter is going to explain it all to you in clear and simple terms.

In the other sections I will give you techniques which you can use immediately. For now let's cover the important fundamentals. Here we go.

# Is There a Difference Between Shyness and Social Anxiety?

The big difference between the two is in **how much they affect your life**. Here are some signs to find out whether you have shyness or social anxiety.

**Signs that you have shyness:**

- You only feel a little bit of anxiety and nervousness in social situations. (But it doesn't stop you from doing things you want to do, like going to parties.)
- You have trouble speaking to people you're intimidated of, like your boss or a guy/girl you find attractive.

- You have trouble talking to people you're not familiar with. However, around people you know well you can probably talk for hours.
- You talk less often or quieter than most people.
- You can function almost normally except for some worry or social awkwardness.
- You may be insecure about your appearance.

**Signs that you have social anxiety:**

- All of the above    and
- Being around people in general makes you feel anxious and uncomfortable.
- You avoid spending any more time around people than you need to. Even if you feel lonely or would like to make friends.
- You often blush, sweat or shake because of your anxiety. Even in everyday situations like having a casual conversation with someone.
- You experience panic attacks. (Sudden fear or extreme nervousness for 10 minutes or more.)
- And, most importantly, your social anxiety prevents you from functioning normally. You don't have friends, you are afraid to go to the store, you can't get a job, and so on.

# Shyness and Social Anxiety Are Fundamentally The Same Thing

The most important thing to know is that **shyness and social anxiety are both simply two different labels** for the same problem. They are the same thing at different levels of seriousness. Social anxiety is the severe form of shyness. Shyness is the "light" form of social anxiety.

Most people do not simply have either shyness or social anxiety. They usually fall somewhere in between the two, as seen in the diagram below.

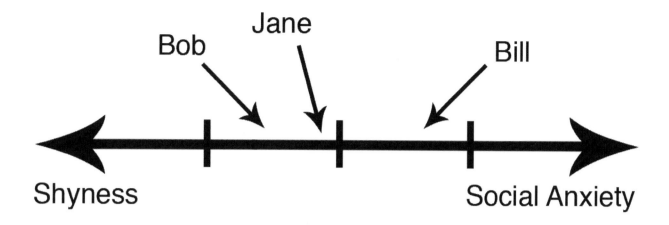

**Figure 1: Different levels of social anxiety**

Although social anxiety will affect someone's life a lot more than shyness will, both issues are rooted in the same basic causes. This means they are also able to be treated in the same way. That's why I can write about both in one system.

However, for some people who are only a little shy, some of the things I talk about in this system are going to be things which they already know how to do, like making eye contact. Feel free to skip the sections which are too basic or don't feel can help you.

> **NOTE: For the sake of faster and better reading, from now on in this book I have <u>shortened</u> both shyness and social anxiety into just "SA".**

Now that you know the difference between shyness and social anxiety, and how they are both really the same thing, it's time to look deeper into it. I'll start by clearing up a few of the myths surrounding SA.

# <u>Myth #1:</u> SA Is An Illness Caused By Genetics Or A Chemical Imbalance

SA is not a real disorder or illness, despite the name sometimes given to it: "social anxiety disorder".

99% of people out there who have SA have nothing physically wrong with their mind or body that needs to be fixed through medication. (Of course, always see your doctor just in case you happen to be in the minority.)

Social anxiety can be fixed, but not by altering your body's chemical balances through medication. Medication helps some people manage their anxiety better, but it will never make it go away. It can only be a temporary fix. To make it go

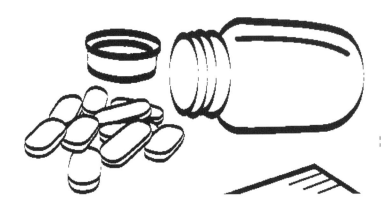

away permanently, you'll need a different approach, which I'll share with you in just a bit.

By the way, the reason why so many people believe this myth is because big pharmaceutical companies want to sell more drugs to people. It's in their best interest to make you think it's a biological problem, instead of a psychological one. Think I'm kidding? Here's what a Harvard professor of medicine has to say about it:

> "If you watch television in the evening, the news shows, it's marketing one drug after the other. And it not only markets the drugs--it markets the medical conditions they are used to treat. It convinces people who watch shows that there is a brand new drug, a miracle drug for every ailment and discontent they can come up with. And so if they are shy, suddenly they have Social Anxiety Disorder and they need Paxil."
>
> **- Dr. Marcia Angell, Harvard Medical Professor**

What scientific studies have found is that drugs used to treat disorders like anxiety or depression are not as effective as the strategy I'm going to teach you in this book.

The drugs (sometimes) work as long as you're taking them, but as soon as you stop, the anxiety or depression comes right back, because you haven't fixed the root of the problem. You only masked the symptoms.

Anti-anxiety medication does help some people when it is used along with the type of strategy I'm going to teach you. **It is most useful for those who have extremely severe anxiety issues, to help them get started on their way to getting better.**

This being said, I'm neither a medical doctor nor a psychiatrist, and nothing in this book should be taken as medical advice.

# Myth #2: SA Is A Personality Trait

This is also a common myth many people with SA believe. When you were young, someone may have told you, "You're shy" or "You're quiet." This assumes that SA is a part of your personality or identity. It's something you were born with or have developed over time to become a part of you, like your hair or feet. But the truth is, SA is not a part of your personality.

**Think about it: Are you anxious or shy all the time?** Are you equally anxious when you're talking to someone new as when you're talking to your closest friend? How about when talking to a group of people versus just one person?

No, you aren't. So what does this mean?

# TRUTH: SA is a Learned Behavior

SA is a learned behavior. It's a set of mental and physical behaviors you've learned to use to **react** to certain situations. The amount and the type of reaction you feel depends on the situation.

Here's a few examples:

- You may not be able to **make conversation** with strangers easily, but there's probably one or two people in your life who you can talk to effortlessly.
- You may not be able to make a speech in front of many people without sweating and shaking, but you can talk to one person comfortably.

- You may not be able to **make eye contact** with someone you are intimidated by (like an authority figure) or someone you are attracted to, but with other people it's much easier.
- You may be **quiet** and hard-to-hear when there's lots of people listening, but when you're in a private room you can speak as loud as you want.

The important thing to understand is that nobody has shyness or anxiety in every area, it always relates to specific situations.

So stop assuming SA is a part of your personality and turning it into an unchangeable identity. Don't say: "That's the way I am." Say: "In this situation…"

SA is a set of thoughts and behaviors you have <u>learned</u> to use in certain social situations. **This also means you can unlearn these thoughts and behaviors and replace them with new ones**. Everything you need to do to unlearn these thoughts and behaviors will be explained a little later in this book.

For now you just need to understand that SA is basically a set of bad habits you've become stuck into. If you can overcome these old habits of thinking and acting a certain way, then your SA will be gone. It's as simple as that.

**SA isn't something you are, it's something you do, sometimes.** It's a learned behavior, a learned reaction - not something you were born with. And SA is always situational, you feel it more or less based on what situation you find yourself in. Therefore, thinking of yourself as a "shy" or "socially anxious" person is the wrong way to look at it.

# The Purpose of SA Is To Avoid Disapproval

**SA is driven by an extreme fear of disapproval.** People who have shyness or social anxiety are scared to death that:

- Someone will criticize or reject them based on their appearance or behavior.
- They will make a negative impression on someone.
- Someone will judge them negatively.

SA is often based on the assumption that you are in some way weak, inferior, inadequate or less good than others, combined with the fear people will notice this (supposedly built-in) defect and disapprove of you. And the disapproval will have very negative consequences for your ability to get on with people and to feel you belong.

Because of their fear of disapproval, people with SA react to situations where they think they will experience disapproval or rejection in the same way that most people would react to real danger. They often even experience physical symptoms like a racing heart, shaking, or sweating.

Your SA is a fear of disapproval. Now I'm going to explain it deeper. Pay attention, because when I realized what I'm about to teach you, it really explained a lot to me and gave me a new perspective on my own SA.

# Probability and Consequences

Isn't it true that in some social situations you only feel a little anxious or shy, and in others you feel very anxious or shy?

The reason why is because when you feel anxiety, **your brain is trying to predict the probability and consequences of disapproval occurring.** In other words, your brain is constantly trying to calculate how likely it is that someone will disapprove/reject/criticize you, and it's also trying to predict how bad the result of the disapproval could be.

Your brain will only make you feel SA if it <u>predicts you are likely</u> to experience disapproval, or that you would be in <u>big trouble</u> if someone disapproved of you. See, it's like your brain is sending you a warning signal when you feel anxiety or shyness, and it sends the warning signal only when it thinks the probability or consequences of disapproval occurring are high. Let me show you what I mean with some real-life examples:

- You probably feel a lot more anxious at the possibility of **talking to a group of people than talking to one person**. Why? It's because your brain thinks if you make a mistake talking in front of many people, then everyone will think you're a fool instead of just one person. The possible consequences of a speech are higher than a one-on-one conversation.

- You also probably feel more anxious **talking to an authority figure** like a police officer or teacher. Why? Although there's not a great risk of them disapproving of you, if they did, your brain thinks the consequences could be severe. Getting a police officer mad could ruin your reputation or even put you in jail. (Especially outside of first-world countries.) The same thing happens with other authority figures like teachers and bosses.

- Most people who have SA have a hard time **talking to people they don't know well**, even over the phone. Why is it that strangers cause so much more anxiety than someone you know well? It's because when you're around people you don't know well, <u>you don't know how they are going to react to you</u>, so your brain makes you become shy and withdrawn. The only time people with SA will be louder and more outgoing is in situations where they are unlikely to experience disapproval. So around close friends and family you know the people well enough to know how they will react to what you do. And you know it won't be with disapproval.

- On the other hand, if you have a parent (or boss or someone else) who is often unpredictably angry or strict, then you may feel more anxiety around them. This is because there's a good chance they may just disapprove of you without reason.

In a nutshell, SA is caused by a fear of disapproval, and the amount of SA you feel is situational. It goes back to what I talked about before – about SA being a situational reaction. And, like you just learned, anxiety is basically a prediction in your brain. The amount of anxiety or shyness increases when your brain predicts there's a high chance of disapproval, or possible severe consequences to the disapproval.

# Why Avoid Disapproval?

Now I'm going to dive deeper into motivations, and WHY do people with SA avoid disapproval? Why do they fear it so much? Where does this fear come from?

After doing much research, the answer I came to was very surprising. Believe it or not, the root of the fear of disapproval actually comes from thousands of years ago, when humans were still cavemen.

See, our brain and basic emotional system is almost the same now as it was a few thousand years ago in caveman times. Evolution happens very slowly. Although some parts of our brains have become very intelligent, other parts of our brains are still working the same way as a caveman's.

**Specifically, the part of the brain which controls fear and anxiety works almost exactly the same as how it worked thousands of years ago**. This primitive part of the brain is called the <u>Amygdala</u>.

# The Amygdala

The Amygdala only has one goal: to keep you alive. Survival is the only priority, as far as it is concerned.

Every animal has a survival instinct wired deep into its psychology. Stay alive, no matter what. This survival instinct is the reason why the human species has survived and evolved for millions of years. Without it we would have become extinct long ago.

**The Amygdala makes you feel fear, anxiety, and stress because it wants to help you avoid danger and stay alive.** The Amygdala is the reason why, when you see a dangerous animal, you immediately want to run away – there's no thinking required. It's also why you probably are scared to go near the edge of a high building. You have an automatic self preservation mechanism built into you. There's no thinking required.

Let me repeat that last bit    When it comes to fear and anxiety, <u>there's no thinking required</u>. Shyness and anxiety is something that happens automatically, it's an instinctual response. It's not rational – nobody chooses to have shyness or social anxiety. It just happens.

This is a "big secret" most people don't know about. **Many, if not most, of our emotions and behaviors are secretly driven by a subconscious, instinctual need to survive.** Most people don't realize how much their emotions and behaviors are being controlled by the primitive survival part of their brain.

## What does this have to do with SA?

Well, we've already established that SA is a fear of disapproval and that our brain has developed to try to help us survive. We also know that much of the "programming" in the brain is still from thousands of years ago when humans had to live in tribes to survive in their hostile environment.

Now imagine if you lived in a tribe back in caveman days. Why would a caveman want to avoid disapproval from his tribe? Because if a caveman's tribe disapproved of him severely, they would kick him out of the tribe. And back in those days, being out in the wilderness on your own meant that you probably wouldn't survive.

**In caveman days, disapproval meant death.** This is why, even to this day when our survival does not depend on other people's approval, we are still driven to avoid disapproval. It's a built-in survival mechanism.

> "The psychoanalysts sometimes state that the root source of all fear is the fear of death. I think that in a way they are right."
>
> **- Kenneth H. Wilson, M.D.**

Knowing the source of SA, you can see that SA is not always a problem. If you were never concerned about being judged or about what other people thought of you, you would probably do things that would get you into trouble. A certain amount of SA protects you from doing things that could lead to severe social consequences.

Everybody has some social anxiety or shyness that affects their behavior. It's why people don't walk down the street yelling and insulting people. It's also why most people drink alcohol at social gatherings to "loosen up". So everyone has some social inhibition, and that's a good thing.

**The problem is that people who have "shyness or social anxiety" take it too far in the other direction.** They are so worried about not getting disapproval, that the quality of their life suffers. The "survival instinct" part of your brain is constantly being triggered even when there is no real threat.

SA becomes a problem when it stops you from doing things you want to do – like making friends, having romantic relationships, getting ahead in your career, saying something in front of the class, and so on. If SA stops you from living the life you want, in other words, then it has definitely become a problem. And I'm here to help you fix that problem.

# Chapter 3
# The "Secret Causes" Of Your SA

**Now that you have a good idea of what SA is and what it isn't, it's time to look at the causes.** This chapter is going to be mostly about the science behind your shyness or social anxiety. You'll get a better understanding of what it is and how it works.

That being said, I'm not going to bore you with long pages of science. I'm also not going to force you to obsess over every detail of your childhood.

Most of the books out there on shyness or social anxiety seem to be written by psychologists who know a lot about how SA works, but don't actually tell you how to overcome it!

> "Pinpointing the nature or origin of your problem may give you insight, but usually fails to change the way you act. This is not surprising."
>
> **- David D. Burns, M.D.**

All I want to do is give you a rough working understanding of your condition. Why? Because when you don't know how your old, outdated emotional system works, then the fear and anxiety feels so real. Knowing how it works allows you to get perspective on your fears and change.

In the other sections I will give you techniques which you can use immediately. For now let's cover the important fundamentals. Here we go.

# Cause #1: Social Learning

Social learning is how we figure out what is "good" or acceptable behavior at a young age. When we are young, we learn by doing things and then looking towards others to see if they approve.

Think about toddlers for example. Most of them don't understand language. If their mom says "Don't do that", they don't actually get the point of the words that she is saying. But what they do understand is **if they are getting a positive or negative reaction** from their parents to what they are doing. We're wired to pick up on CUES of approval or disapproval almost since the time we're born.

This is social learning and it's the main way people's behavior is shaped by those around them when they are growing up. Since we are hardwired to believe that disapproval is a threat to our survival, we would slowly stop doing things that resulted in disapproval.

For example    If a toddler was about to touch an electrical socket and his mom said "DON'T DO THAT!", then the toddler is a lot less likely to try to touch the electrical socket in the future. Social learning is generally a good thing, because it is a strategy developed by evolution to try to keep us alive as we're growing up.

## How does this relate to your SA?

So, if at a young age you tried to step up and be confident and your parents told you "be quiet," or "behave" or "act nice" or something similar, then you would learn that confidence isn't acceptable behavior. You wouldn't do that again. You would learn that acting in a shy or introverted way was the best way to get acceptance from the people around you. And social acceptance is one of the very basic human needs.

# Trying To Be Confident Is Actually Painful...

In fact, a recent University of California, Los Angeles study found that this negative social feedback activates the same area of the brain as when we feel pain.

So, just like when you put your hand on the stove as a child and you learned very quickly not to do that again because of the pain, you can also start to avoid social situations that might result in the pain of disapproval. Trying to be confident is actually painful.

Trying to be confident and the center of attention is now seen by a certain part of your mind as being a behavior that will result in you getting disapproval. Which is painful.

**Here's Social Learning in a nutshell:** We are constantly looking at how other people react to what we do in order to figure out what is "good" behavior. What is the behavior that we should repeat in the future? What is the behavior that we are punished or rewarded for with disapproval or acceptance?

Simple. And this happens ALL THE TIME. In every interaction that you have ever had, you have looked at other people's reactions to what you are doing to see if it was "good". And you don't even know you were doing it 99% of the time. Everybody does this, subtly, subconsciously, and automatically.

# "If Everyone Does This, Why Doesn't Everyone Have SA?"

People with SA are born with a genetic trait that makes them see other people's responses <u>with greater intensity</u> than a regular person. It's a specific type of sensitivity.

In other words, other people's disapproval does not have the same emotional impact on regular people as on people who eventually develop SA. So a lot of negative reactions regular people get don't register in their brain. This lets them seem to care a lot less about what other people around them think of them than people with SA.

Okay, get it? So, because you saw negative reactions when you tried to be confident as a child, you slowly developed negative feelings to social situations. This is what made you become shy or socially anxious.

In summary, your SA was caused by a combination of you being genetically predisposed to developing the condition (increased sensitivity to other's reactions), combined with being in the wrong place at the wrong time (getting disapproval to being confident).

# Negative, Critical, Controlling...

In fact, one observation that a famous psychologist made was that people with shyness or social anxiety tended to be raised by someone who was negative, critical, and controlling of them while they were growing up. Think about that    Was one of your parents or other authority figures very negative, critical and controlling of you when you were growing up? This can cause someone to develop excessive inhibition to avoid the negative criticism. You become shy to avoid "setting the person off", so to speak.

I VERY often hear stories from people who tell me they only started to become socially anxious when they were bullied or excluded at some point in their life. Maybe their parents decided to move, and at the new school they didn't fit in right away and felt not accepted. It's another form of social learning.

# Learning by Example

Another possible cause of your social anxiety could be learning by example - maybe you had parents or an older sibling that had SA growing up and you were just imitating their behavior.

Kids are generally wired to imitate others as they are growing up. You'll even see this happening if you watch documentaries of wild animals raising their babies. Kids learn how to live and survive in the world through copying and imitating the older people. So if everyone around you growing up was shy or socially withdrawn, then you may have been accidentally programmed that this is the "normal" way to live. Making outside friends and having a social life would be totally unknown territory to you, and therefore outside of your believed "realm of possibility".

Now let's move on to the second possible cause of SA, which is

# Cause #2: Toxic Shame

If you're only a little shy, then this section may not apply to you. But I believe most people who have more severe shyness or social anxiety had it start with something called toxic shame.

What is toxic shame? It's similar to shame, but worse. When you feel regular shame, you are ashamed of something you did. When you feel toxic shame, you are <u>ashamed of yourself as a person</u>. This type of shame usually takes over your life. So how do you know if you have toxic shame?

# Effects Of Toxic Shame

In general, toxic shame can make you feel inadequate, not good enough, unworthy of love. It'll make you isolate and withdraw yourself from people. Since you're almost always focused on all of the parts of you which are "not good enough", it can also make you depressed.

When you have toxic shame, you think they have to hide your defects or perceived flaws from other people to avoid getting rejected. Here are some examples:

- **Have you ever thought you were ugly?** I think the majority of people who have SA struggle with insecurities about their appearance. If you are always checking how you look in mirrors or feeling bad about your appearance, then you're not alone. I was like this for many years.

- **Do you ever feel like nobody likes you because you're boring or uninteresting?** Many people with SA also feel like this – as if nobody would like them if they really got to know them.

- **Do you feel like you have to "hide" your true self from people**, especially when you don't know them well? This includes your life, opinions, interests, and general personality.

- **Are you uncomfortable with closeness or intimacy with other people?** This causes you to withdraw and isolate yourself from others. It makes forming a real and close connection with people very difficult    which is maybe the reason why you haven't been able to have many friends or a girlfriend/boyfriend up until now.

- **Do you think that you just don't know how to talk to people?** Again, this is toxic shame, and it causes you to avoid trying to improve your social skills. You feel like you are fundamentally different in some way, like you are unfixable. I hope that since you are listening to this system, you believe that there's at least a possibility for improvement.

- **Are you obsessed with hiding the symptoms of your SA?** For example, wanting to hide sweating, shaking, blushing, or a rapid heartbeat from other people. You're afraid of other people finding out that you feel nervous and you always want to sound 100% confident. It's another way of believing that people would reject you if they were exposed to the real you, your real feelings at this moment.

In all of these examples, there's usually some specific thing about you which you think is your defect. All of these "defects" are things which you think are causing your SA. You feel anxiety the most when you think people are about to notice or "uncover" the defect.

The thing you need to understand is that **the thing you feel ashamed about really doesn't matter that much**. You don't have social anxiety because your appearance or personality is bad, or anything else. The way toxic shame works is that it will find something about you to be ashamed about.

So it's not that you were ugly first and then started feeling anxious about it. No. The shame came first and started distorting the way you see yourself. No matter who they are, people who have SA will find something flawed about them to feel ashamed about.

One example of this is if you look on forums for people who have social anxiety, you'll find a lot of people asking if they're ugly     and then when you look at their photo they look like a normal person, and often they may even be more attractive than average. Or they think they are a loser with an uninteresting life, without realizing that most people's lives aren't filled with exciting things everyday. It's a distortion of the way you see yourself.

**Another common "defect" is believing that if people found out you have a lonely, boring life, they would be repulsed by you.** I remember back when I had very bad social anxiety, if someone asked me what I did on the weekend or last night, I would immediately become defensive or awkward and try to lie. This particular belief is really bad because it keeps you trapped. If you are afraid to expose your real self and life to people, then it's almost impossible to connect and make friends. And if you don't have friends, you feel ashamed of yourself and hide away. It's a vicious circle.

For now I'm just pointing out the issues. I'll show you how to fix the shame later in this system, in the part called "Changing The Way You Think."

# Where Does Toxic Shame Come From?

It is caused by a hostile environment growing up. **When people are very young, they have a need for unconditional love and acceptance.** When they don't receive it, then they may develop toxic shame.

The most common cause is careless, abusive, or overprotective parents, since the parents are usually the biggest influence on a child. But it could also be caused by other relatives, authority figures, or even school bullies.

For now I'll focus on toxic shame caused by a parent. Many people who have social anxiety faced some type of parental neglect or abandonment when they were young. This can range from your parents getting a divorce to being away at work a lot, to pretty much anything

- You were hungry and no one fed you.
- You cried and no one held you.
- You were lonely and no one payed attention to you.
- Your parent got angry at you, neglected you, shamed you, hit you, didn't want you.
- Your parent left and didn't come back in a timely manner.
- Your parent put unrealistic expectations on you.

**See, when a child is young, their mind works in a very self-centered way.** They think that they are the cause of everything that happens in the world. So if as a child you saw your parent not paying enough attention to you, you would automatically assume that it's somehow your fault. Even if they were actually trying to be good parents, and their behavior had nothing to do with you.

You would look at their behavior and automatically believe that you're not good enough or worthy. You would start to feel ashamed of yourself and become obsessed with trying to gain love and acceptance, and avoid disapproval. You would feel like it wasn't safe or acceptable for you to be just as you are.

# "Why Don't Most People Have Toxic Shame?"

One of the facts of life is that nobody's perfect. Since nobody had perfect parents growing up, almost everybody had some of the rejection or abandonment experiences I listed before happen to them during childhood.

So then why does only a small percentage of people develop toxic shame and SA?

It's because of what I mentioned before – **people who have SA tend to have a greater sensitivity to experiences of disapproval and rejection.** They also tend to interpret these types of experiences as being their fault much more than others.

It's important to realize that someone who has shyness or social anxiety does not always have toxic shame. It's just something that is very common with people who have more serious cases of social anxiety or trouble forming close relationships.

Growing up I definitely had a bad case of toxic shame. It began probably around the time when I was 3 years old. My parents opened a fast food restaurant and worked there very long hours for 7 days a week. In my child's mind, I saw the sudden decrease of attention as being a form of abandonment or rejection. This is about the time when my shyness really took off and turned into severe social anxiety.

Does this mean that they "caused" my toxic shame? Not really, it was my child's self-centered mind that interpreted the event as "they don't spend as much time with me because I'm no good." (This wasn't something I was consciously thinking, by the way. It was more of an unconscious belief that revealed itself through extreme social anxiety, social withdrawal, and insecurity.)

---

### The Interpretation, Not The Event, Causes Toxic Shame

---

This is a very important point: It was <u>my mind's interpretation</u> of the event that caused the shame, not the event itself. **Whenever something happens to you, there's always the event, and then there's the personal interpretation you put around the event.** Unfortunately, if you have toxic shame, the interpretation that created your current beliefs was formed when your mind was still immature.

My older brother, on the other hand, didn't develop toxic shame or SA because his mind didn't interpret them needing to be away from home as being his fault.

# Psychological Imprinting

As a side note, there's a whole area of psychology that talks about "imprinting." Imprinting is the idea that people are particularly sensitive or vulnerable to developing attitudes and beliefs at certain stages of life.

**The most common time for people to have beliefs "imprinted" into them is when they are very young.** When you are very young, you are at a vulnerable stage of life. Both positive and negative beliefs can be very easily imprinted into you at this point in your life which will then be hard to "unwire" later.

By the way, this is why most people believe in whatever religion their parents believe in. They were exposed to it before their rational mind was developed enough to decide whether to accept or reject it. And once a belief is imprinted, whether it's toxic shame or religious   it becomes very difficult to see things from another perspective.

# Unwiring Toxic Shame

Now, lets get started on the first step of unwiring toxic shame.

**If you think you have toxic shame, try to remember when and where it started.**

- It may have been some embarrassing or humiliating incident. (Maybe a religious parent caught you looking at porn and you became very ashamed of yourself.)

- It may have been someone pressuring you with unrealistic expectations, or rejecting you for who you were. (Maybe someone constantly compared you to a sibling and made you compete for love and attention.)

- It may have been some experience of abandonment. (Maybe you started to feel toxic shame after your parents divorced and you stopped seeing one of them as often.)

Here's a good pointer: **When you remember the experience, do you feel a wave of shame and bad emotions come over you now?** That's a dead giveaway of a toxic shame event because it shows you that you have a negative emotional charge attached to the memory. It's kind of showing you that it's a traumatic incident.

It may even have been something that you can't even remember. But if you can remember it, try to see how the event itself did not cause the shame. It was <u>your interpretation</u> of the event which caused the shame. You saw the abandonment, rejection, or humiliation as being your fault, when it was really caused by external factors.

# Reinterpreting Past Events

**One of the first steps to overcoming toxic shame is learning to reinterpret events in a healthier way.** Blaming or putting the responsibility on other people for your current problems is a useless strategy. It's useless because it doesn't accomplish anything, and will just make you feel more helpless about your life.

So the thing to do after reading this chapter and getting some insight into what caused your SA is to take responsibility and see how your interpretations caused your toxic shame. Now, I'm not really saying it's your fault. When you were a kid you weren't able to control your interpretations, but now you can. So now you're able to take responsibility and have control. And I'll show you how.

In fact, let's use some of the examples mentioned in this chapter so I can show you how this reinterpretation is done:

| Event | Old Interpretation | New Interpretation |
|---|---|---|
| **Parent doesn't spend as much time with you because of divorce or work.** | They don't like me. | They weren't in love with other parent anymore or had to work more to support me. |
| **Relative caught me looking at porn.** | I'm a bad person. I should feel guilty and ashamed of myself. | They were brought up in a more conservative era. |
| **Someone constantly compared you to others and seemed to like you better when you performed well in school/sports.** | I need to become better to be accepted. | They thought putting high standards was the best way to teach you how to be successful. Maybe their parents did it to them. |

You should really take the time to create your own chart like this one. List the event, your old interpretation that caused toxic shame, and the new interpretation which doesn't blame the person, but tries to empathize with why they acted the way they did, and how it had little to do with your worth as a person.

Notice how you have to take a good look at how your old beliefs were formed irrationally, and work on rebuilding them rationally. Notice also how all of the new interpretations do not blame the other person (whether that be your parents, a bully, or anyone else) for your problems. The new interpretations focus on compassion for whoever's behavior may have caused your toxic shame. This strategy empowers you to let go of the shame, and avoids useless anger and negativity. If someone may have abandoned or rejected you or treated you unfairly, try to understand why they acted that way. Maybe their own upbringing caused them to act this way or they really believed they were acting in your own best interest.

We'll talk a lot more about how to overcome toxic shame in the later chapters on changing the way you think. For now just keep this technique for reinterpreting past events in mind.

There are many ways SA forms. The most important thing to remember is that it's almost always a combination of genetics and environment, not one or the other.

Now how to fix it? Let me show you

# Chapter 4
# The Breakthrough Scientific Approach To Get Rid Of SA

Okay, so let's review what you've learned so far

1.  First, shyness and social anxiety are both labels for the same basic problem. In this book we'll call them both SA. SA is an extreme fear of disapproval.
2.  Second, SA is not genetic or a personality trait. It's a learned behavior you use to react to certain social situations. This means you can also unlearn this behavior.
3.  Third, SA was caused either through social learning at a young age or through toxic shame.

In this chapter, I'm going to introduce you to the basic strategy of how to "unlearn" SA. This method is based on tested science and proven to work in my own experience and the experiences of literally hundreds of my students over the past few years.

The strategy starts with a scientific discovery called neuroplasticity

# Neuroplasticity – The Discovery That Shocked The World Of Science and Psychology

What is neuroplasticity? It's the idea that the brain can change and "rewire" itself at any time.

See, up until recently, scientists always believed that the brain stayed the same after childhood for your whole life. They thought if you grew up with SA, then you couldn't change it. You were stuck with it.

This long-accepted "truth" of science was turned upside down around 2004, when scientists began to study and look more closely at the brain. Using new machines that could look at the individual neurons in the brain, they were shocked to discover that <u>it is possible</u> to change the very structure and wiring of your brain. Not just in childhood, but at any point in your life.

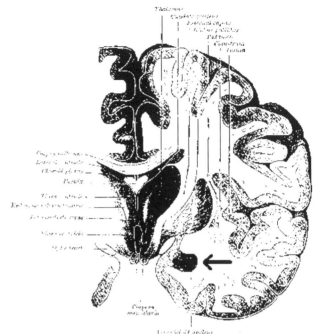

Figure 2: The little arrow near the bottom right points out the amygdala.

**What this means for you is that SA can be changed by "rewiring" your brain, even if you've lived with it your whole life.**

Do you find this hard to believe? Actually, I'm not saying anything new or shocking. This process of "rewiring" the brain's old ways of thinking is the basis of all forms of successful therapy when it comes to anxiety or depression.

> "The discovery of neuroplasticity, that our thoughts can change the structure and function of our brains, even into old age, is the most important breakthrough in our understanding of the brain in four hundred years."
>
> **- Dr. Norman Doidge**

So how can you actually use neuroplasticity to "rewire" your brain? To explain this to you, I'll first have to tell you a bit more about that part of the brain called the Amygdala.

# Your Amygdala: Anxiety Control Center In Your Brain

The Amygdala is the most important part of your brain when it comes to SA. You probably remember about it from the first chapter in this book. In case you don't, here's a quick refresher

The Amygdala is one of the most primitive parts of your brain. It makes you feel fear and anxiety because it wants to help you avoid danger and stay alive. You can almost think of the Amygdala as being your survival instincts.

**The Amygdala works by connecting a certain thing/stimulus to danger.** For example, if you are afraid of spiders, this means your Amygdala has connected spiders to danger in your mind. And it works the same way with any other fear, like height, public speaking or whatever.

The Amygdala is a primitive part of your brain that's designed to keep you safe from perceived threats. By primitive, I mean that the Amygdala isn't a part of your conscious, reasoning brain. It operates on a more basic level, underneath your conscious control.

**All the Amygdala does is automatically link pain or danger to certain experiences and pleasure to others based on what it has witnessed in the past. It predicts danger, and makes you feel fear/anxiety in advance as a sort of "early warning system."**

There are two main ways the Amygdala works:

1) Through predicting danger or

2) Through responding to immediate danger.

# Predicting Danger

This one is pretty straightforward. When your brain can imagine something you fear happening in the near future, then it will make you feel anxiety.

Let's use public speaking as an example. Right now, imagine you were sitting in your class or at your work waiting to be called up to say a few words in front of everybody. **Take 20-30 seconds to really picture a scene in your mind where you would be forced to go up and talk in front of people.** Who would be there? Your boss? Your relatives? That girl or guy you like?

Now think about how it would be like sitting in that chair as you wait to be called up. You begin to feel the anxiety coming up. Your hands start to feel cold and clammy, your stomach tightens, you feel sweat dripping from your armpits, your breathing becomes quicker and shallower.

As you wait nervously, you count the number of people in the room who will be watching you. How many are there? A dozen? Fifteen? Twenty?

Their loud voices fill the room as you sit quietly, trying to rehearse what you're going to say. You become painfully self conscious of every little movement your feet and hands make, and wish you could look in a mirror just for a second to check how you look. You aren't sure where you should put your hands anymore, and you feel very tense. You can feel your heart beating out of control. You hope people won't notice how nervous and sweaty you are. You hope the teacher or boss won't tell you to speak up because you're being quiet

I hope you get the point by now. When you were reading the example above, did you actually start to feel a little anxious? That's the power of imagination. Just reading about the situation made you start to imagine yourself in it, which "tricked" your Amygdala into making you anxious even thought there's no real danger present – you're just sitting here reading a book!

The idea behind this example is to show you how imagination or anticipation is a big cause of anxiety. **Your imagination actually causes you to feel anxiety as if you were**

**actually in the situation you are imagining.** When someone has severe social anxiety, they experience this type of anticipatory anxiety all the time. Before they go to the store, before they walk past someone on the street, before they call someone on the phone before they do almost anything!

For a shy person, this type of anxiety is usually less frequent, maybe before asking someone on a date, going into a job interview, going to a party, or speaking in front of a large group of people.

# Responding to Immediate Danger

The other way the Amygdala works is through responding to danger right in front of you. If the Amygdala detects danger, it immediately activates a **"fight or flight" response**. It's like you have gone into a type of "survival mode."

Maybe you have heard of this before if you watch any nature documentaries. If you haven't heard of the "fight or flight" response, then I'll explain it quickly.

Most animal's bodies have an automatic response when they come into contact with possible danger. For example, if a deer suddenly saw a lion in the wild, its body would immediately flood with adrenaline and other chemicals. This response is designed to make the animal stronger or faster temporarily so that it could either fight the lion or get away safely.

The chemicals of the "fight or flight" work through increasing your heart rate and breathing, redirecting the circulation of your blood to the main muscles, and shutting down the higher functioning of your brain. **All of this is done to preserve energy for what is most important in the moment: survival.**

# SA Symptoms And The "Fight Or Flight" Response

The "fight or flight" response is what causes a lot of the actual symptoms of SA. The most noticeable symptoms are the <u>physical symptoms</u> like:

- rapid heartbeat,
- trembling/shaking,
- shortness of breath,
- sweating,
- cold hands, etc

There are also some <u>mental symptoms</u> of the "fight or flight" response. The most interesting one for me is the fact that it causes people who have SA to "run out of things to say."

If you have SA, then this problem should probably be very familiar to you. Think about the last time you walked into a job interview or talked to someone you found attractive or intimidating. Did you find that you had to struggle with what to say?

**The reason why this happens is because, when you are anxious, the "fight or flight" mode also shuts down some of the higher-level functioning of the brain.** Your Amygdala is one of the more primitive parts of your brain, and when it is triggered, it redirects "brainpower" from the other parts of your brain which are more useful at talking about things in an interesting and creative way.

This is why, when you are feeling anxious around someone, it becomes so difficult to carry on simple conversations or think of what to say. On the other hand, if you are relaxed and comfortable around someone, then you may be able to carry on hours-long conversations with them without worrying about running out of things to talk about.

I'm sure you can relate to this. So the main cure to "running out of things to say" and avoiding awkward silences is to learn how to become comfortable and relaxed. There are other conversational "tricks" I'll teach you later, but this is the foundation. And the way to become comfortable and relaxed is to rewire the Amygdala so it doesn't set off the "fight or flight" response.

Makes sense?

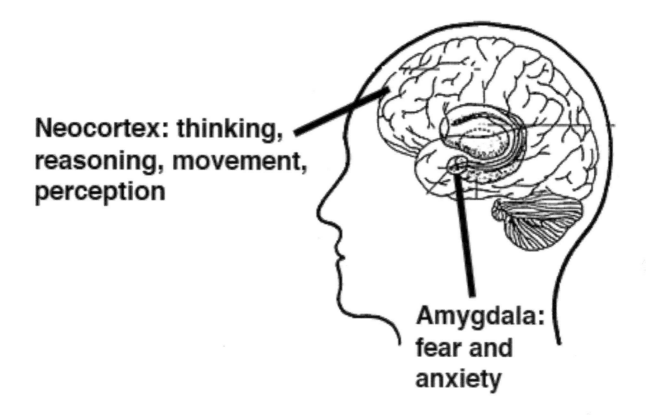

**Figure 3: The Amygdala shuts down some of the higher functioning of the brain (the Neocortex) when you feel anxiety.**

So now you know roughly how the Amygdala works. It either responds to immediate danger by creating a "fight or flight" response or it predicts/imagines future danger and causes you to feel anxiety in advance.

The next question is: how can you stop your Amygdala from seeing something as being dangerous? If you think about it, the answer to this question is actually the key to overcoming SA. So here's the answer

# Experiences Are The Answer, Not Intellectual Knowledge

The Amygdala works through emotional memory. In other words, it works by interpreting past experiences. You are afraid of disapproval because some past experiences (or your interpretation of them) caused you to view disapproval as being dangerous to your survival. This is where either social learning or toxic shame started it all.

This is an important point to grasp, because it means **you can only un-learn any anxiety by showing your Amygdala through new experiences that there's nothing to be afraid of.** You can't use logical, rational arguments to change what your Amygdala knows to be true through experience or memory.

Let me give you an example. Have you ever tried to be confident before a social situation and tried telling yourself "What's the worst that can happen?" How well did that work out? Probably not too well. How about any other logical reasons you tried to tell yourself not to feel anxious?

This is the problem with a lot of advice out there on overcoming shyness or social anxiety. Someone who has never felt shy in their life will write "you really just have to ask yourself what's the worst that can happen!" or they will write "Think about it: what have you got to lose?".

They think if you can just see how irrational it is to have SA, then you will magically stop. Of course, what they don't know is that most people who have SA are actually pretty smart. And they already know their behavior is irrational. They know there's no real reason to be afraid of what other people think. Yet they still feel the anxiety and nervousness. That's part of what makes SA so frustrating.

# "Proof, Not Promises"

**Logical thought doesn't overcome SA because anxiety and shyness is not caused by the rational, thinking part of your brain.** It is caused by your Amygdala. And you cannot simply talk your Amygdala out of reacting to something that it has learned to identify as painful. You can't just learn some new piece of knowledge and "think your way out of your condition".

The only way to change the Amygdala's reactions is through exposure to the feared stimulus combined with an experience that teaches the Amygdala that nothing bad happens. In other words, your brain wants "proof, not promises."

Acquiring information itself is passive. Experiencing is active. When you 'experience', something happens inside your nervous system and your midbrain. New 'engrams' and 'neural' patterns are recorded in the gray matter of your brain."

**- Maxwell Maltz, M.D., F.I.C.S.**

Do you remember how we talked about Neuroplasticity at the beginning of the chapter and how it is a way to "rewire" the brain? Well, this is the secret of neuroplasticity you have to rewire your brain using experiences.

This is not just A way to overcome SA, it's THE way, THE ONLY WAY. Because it fixes the problem of SA at the core of where it started. So I'll repeat:

**The ONLY way to change the amygdala's learned reactions is through exposure to the feared stimulus in a way that teaches it that nothing bad happens.**

Your Amygdala works through emotional memory. So you have to change the emotions surrounding your memories. And you have to create new memories wrapped in positive and relaxed memories instead of fear and anxiety.

You have to slowly desensitize yourself to social situations and your Amygdala will start to realize that there's nothing to fear. This can only be accomplished with A LOT OF repetition combined with changing how you think and behave on a core level.

But it's not just about getting more exposure to social situations. If that was the case then no one would have SA. It's also about getting <u>the right type</u> of exposure, because it's possible to keep pushing yourself into social situations and only reinforce your SA. I struggled with SA for many years, pushing myself into social situations without making any progress at all, until I figured out the right approach.

So what exactly is the right approach    how do you get "the right type" of exposure? That's what the next chapter is going to be about.

# Chapter 5
# Exposure: The Method For Overcoming Anxiety

In this section, I want to show you the key method that will permanently remove all of your SA. This is not just a method, it's the ONLY method to retrain your Amygdala to show it there's nothing to fear in social situations.

Once you retrain your Amygdala, your brain will stop predicting danger from possible disapproval, so you will stop having anxiety.

## Avoidance Maintains Anxiety

When someone feels uncomfortable, nervous, or afraid, the natural tendency is to try to feel better in any way possible. If their fear is being triggered by a particular object or situation, the easiest way to get rid of the fear is to escape from the situation or to avoid the situation altogether. These types of behaviors are called <u>avoidance behaviors</u>.

**Avoidance behaviors can help you not feel anxiety and fear in the short term, but in the long term they help to maintain your anxiety because they prevent your subconscious mind (your Amygdala) from learning that a situation is safe.**

Avoidance stops your brain from getting used to being in certain situations. Like the first time you tried to swim, you were probably tense and uptight. But, over time, you got used to the feeling of being in the water to the point where you could actually relax. And once you were relaxed, then it became possible to focus on learning the technique and learning how to swim. If you had avoided the water then the fear wouldn't have gone away by itself. So from this point forward it is essential for you to continually face your fears instead of avoiding them.

# Fear Is Your Friend

There are so many people running away from their fears. They are constantly avoiding what they fear. Trying to find pills to take away the anxiety. Looking for ways to distract themselves.

Little do they know that fear not only helps them improve their life, but it's actually their greatest ally. **Fear is like a compass that points you towards the life you want.** All of your deepest desires are fear-ridden, from approaching someone you're attracted to, to starting a new business, to conquering your social anxieties. Whenever you feel fear, you know that you are going after what you truly want and growing as a person.

If you use fear as a guide for your actions, you will find something amazing happening. After you do something many times you fear, slowly, the fear will disappear. In psychology this process is called habituation or progressive desensitization. The thing you used to fear now becomes commonplace and you wonder in disbelief what you were so afraid of in the first place.

**It is essential you let fear guide you to your desired life but not overwhelm you.** It's bittersweet to find that fear is your ally in this. All those years of trying to avoid it, you realize that it actually tells you something positive about yourself.

Fear is not something to be avoided. Fear is your friend. A revolutionary thought.

# DIWA - Do It While Afraid

Many people with SA waste a lot of time thinking about ways to destroy fear, as if fear is the enemy. They look for medication, hypnosis tapes, or they seek that one last piece of knowledge that will make all of their fears disappear.

From now on, don't try to get rid of your fears before entering social situations. Instead, make it your policy to do it while afraid. DIWA for short. Ironically enough, this is the only way to get rid of your fears permanently.

Haven't you done anything while afraid? Have you ever jumped in a pool while thinking the water will be cold? If you think long and hard you will find you have done many things in your life while afraid. Not only that, you accomplished your proudest achievements, scared.

# Focus On Changing Your Actions, Not Your Feelings

One of the most profound concepts in psychology is the fact that when you do something (actions), then your emotions follow along behind. So if you wait around to feel good or feel non-anxious, you'll be waiting forever. *(I'm paraphrasing this from a therapist called Dr. Thomas A. Richards.)*

If you are scared of making eye contact with people when you walk past them, that fear isn't going to go away until you first start making eye contact in spite of that fear. You need to start DOING, and then you will BECOME.

I go by one mantra: **"acknowledge feelings and take appropriate action."** Say to yourself that you are afraid, but that you will do it anyway. Don't let the fear stop you. Don't try to make it go away either. Just watch your fear in a detached way. Recognize that it's just a chemical reaction in your body. If you observe it and act anyways, fear will lose its paralyzing grip.

Fear doesn't go away by learning about it. You would think by this time, having studied so much about fear and anxiety, and the psychology behind them, that I wouldn't be afraid of anything. Nope. I am still afraid. It's just that I'm afraid of different things now. I suspect I will be for as long as I live. But this is okay. Continually "leaning into your fears" is a healthy part of life and a great way to grow as a person.

> Courage is not the lack of fear. It is acting in spite of it.
>
> **- Mark Twain**

# Trying and Failing is Better Than Not Trying

Sometimes when you are faced with a potentially anxious situation, you will feel yourself wanting to avoid it. Avoidance usually comes as a "tug" or urge to run away from a situation. For example, if you spot someone you know walking towards you in the distance, you may get an urge to cross the street to avoid them or to turn into a side street.

**Whenever you feel this "tug" of avoidance, go against it.** Use your willpower or discipline, or whatever you want to call it. Don't fight the feelings inside you and try to make them go away. Instead just accept that you are experiencing some emotions that you can't control, and make your feet move to face the situation anyways. Like my mantra goes: "acknowledge feelings and take appropriate action."

Do the thing you feel least like doing. Sometimes you won't be able to. It'll seem like you have no control over yourself when trying to face certain situations. It'll feel like your feet are moving themselves away from it. That's okay, all it means is that you have to start smaller and build your way up. The important thing is to get into the daily habit of facing, rather than avoiding, the things which cause you to feel anxiety.

If you keep to the habit of facing your fears daily, you'll find that you never regret facing your fears. Even if something doesn't go well, you still feel a sense of pride and accomplishment for stepping up. It's the times when you avoid your fears that make you feel bad.

# "Exposure Doesn't Work For Me!"

I always get some people telling me: "I've been going to school/work and getting exposure for years. It hasn't done anything for my anxiety."

The reason why exposure does nothing for some people is because they do it the wrong way. **If you do exposure the wrong way, your Amygdala won't unlearn the anxiety.** That's why it's ESSENTIAL that you follow the guidelines I lay out in the next few pages.

Believe me, I went to school for years and years with the same amount of crippling shyness and social anxiety. It was only when I started doing the things I will teach you in the rest of this book that I began to transform my social anxiety.

The first thing you have to do is

# Eliminate Partial Avoidance And Safety Behaviors

It's not enough to physically step into the situation that makes you anxious. You have to stop avoiding it in every way possible.

Many people with SA try to decrease their anxiety when in a stressful situation by avoiding certain parts of the situation that are particularly frightening. What they don't realize is that this type of "partial avoidance" is almost as bad as completely avoiding the situation. I'll give examples of what I'm talking about in a minute.

Partial avoidance is bad for the same reason that avoidance is bad. In the short term, when someone does partial avoidance or safety behaviors, it lowers their anxiety. But in the long term, these habits actually maintain anxiety because they stop you from facing it fully. Since you never face the situations you fear head-on, your brain never gets the chance to unlearn its anxiety and learn that the situation is safe.

**Here are the three most common types of partial avoidance:**

# 1. Alcohol/drugs/medication

These are effective at reducing anxiety in the short term, but actually maintain your anxiety in the long term. If you drink alcohol at every social gathering you attend, then your brain will never be able to learn that social gatherings are safe.

Some people do require medication (see a doctor) but usually their therapist's goal is to continually cut back the dosage so the patient can slowly get used to being in situations and not require any anxiety medication at all. So the point of the medication is just to make it easier to get started on the long-term permanent strategy I'm teaching you here.

The same guidelines can be used for alcohol. If you currently have to get very drunk at social gatherings, next time cut down by a significant amount. (By the way, if you don't even get invited to any parties right now, don't worry. We'll cover that later.)

Keeping an anxiety pill in your pocket "just in case" is also a safety behavior. It makes sense to have a safety net "just in case", but it actually works against you because in the long run you will ALWAYS need that anxiety pill to be there.

So these things which appear to help you in the short term actually become a crutch that holds you back if your end goal is to eliminate your SA permanently.

# 2. Restricting Your Behavior

Whenever you are getting exposure for your anxiety, always ask yourself "what am I trying to accomplish here?"

If you want to be able to have fun at parties in the future, then you can't really expect to simply show up to a party, spend the whole time standing in the corner and make your anxiety get better. If you want to become more confident in class, then you can't just sit there quietly, not talking to anyone, not raising your hand to ask a question. In the beginning that may be okay, but you have to be careful about not creating new comfort zones.

You have to continually be trying out more risky behaviors that are outside of your comfort zone. Whether that be eye contact, asking people simple questions, starting to carry longer conversations, starting to speak a little louder, and so on. I'll talk more about this in a few pages.

Whenever you catch yourself restricting your behavior in some way, you know that you're partially avoiding the situation. This can be anything from avoiding eye contact with the people around you, only talking to a "safe" person (someone you know well), or only going to "safe" places.

# 3. Mental Distraction

Another common problem (and this was a HUGE issue for me) is going into situations that cause you to have anxiety, but then mentally distancing yourself from them. This usually happens through daydreaming or getting lost in thought.

**Stay mentally involved with the situation.** You have to actually be present, stay engaged, and focused on what's happening right in front of you.

I'll teach you specific techniques on how to deal with this in the section called "Mindfulness and Being Present". But for now just try to keep your focus on the external world and on other people and start noticing when you begin drifting off into your own little world. Every time you catch yourself daydreaming when you should be socializing, bring your attention back to the present. Keep your attention on the immediate situation you are in.

It's okay to like to think, (as you can probably tell from this system so far, I love to think about abstract ideas all the time). But you have to **recognize the appropriate time to stop using thinking and talking to yourself as an excuse to not talk to other people.** It's a comfortable habit that you have to break to overcome SA, just like people who want to lose weight have to break the comfortable habit of eating junk food.

A good thing to do if you are in a group is to **make small comments** every minute or so. Say "yeah" or "right" or "I know what you mean." This will help you stay involved in what is happening and avoid drifting off into your thoughts and not saying anything.

You'll be amazed at how much easier it is to make conversation when you simply focus your attention and practice being genuinely interested in what is being talked about. (When most people make conversation, this is how they are able to always have something new to say – their attention is completely immersed in what is being talked about.)

# Anxiety is Necessary

What do all of the partial avoidance and safety behaviors have in common? They are all trying to lower the level of anxiety you feel in some way. But here's the shocker

The point of exposure is to EXPOSE yourself to the anxiety in order to show your brain that there's nothing to be afraid of. **As a rule, if you don't feel anxiety when you do it, then it's not real exposure.** You won't get much lasting benefit from it.

You have to ask yourself: is it worth it to suffer some short term anxiety and discomfort in order to live the remaining decades of your life with much less overall anxiety and the types of relationships you desire?

If it is, then aim to expose yourself to anxiety. Expose yourself to the thing that makes you anxious. You should feel the anxiety and discomfort rising inside of your body. Now here's what you do next

# Stay in the Situation
# Until Anxiety Drops

Here's a VERY IMPORTANT part of exposure therapy. **Whenever you enter an anxiety-causing situation, you have to stay in it long enough for your anxiety levels to drop noticeably.** Here's an example diagram of what a typical exposure session will feel like:

\

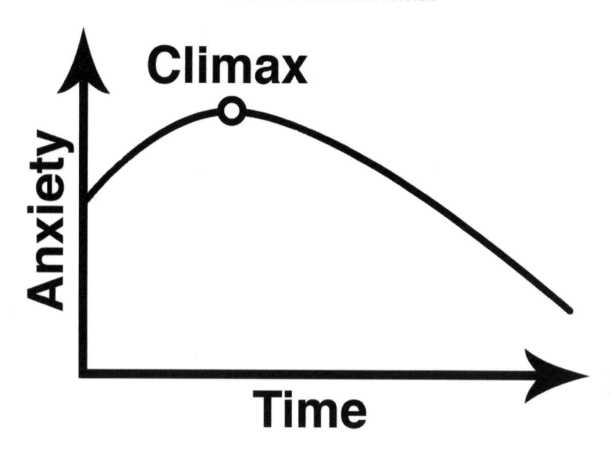

**Let me break this diagram down for you.**

1.  When you first enter the social situation you will feel very anxious. The feelings of anxiety will start to increase and you'll REALLY want to leave the situation.

2.  Don't leave unless you're feeling completely overwhelmed. Seriously    don't leave. Instead, stay in the situation until you have passed the worst of the anxiety.

3.  Wait until you are past the "climax" or peak of your anxiety before you leave the situation. Take a look at the diagram again.

Now, I know what you're probably thinking. "But didn't you just tell me not to try to lower the anxiety I feel? How is my anxiety going to go down if I shouldn't try to lower it?"

When you are getting exposure to social situations, you DO need to lower the amount of anxiety you feel. However, trying to lower your anxiety through either partial avoidance or safety behaviors (the way most people with anxiety try to do it) is the wrong way to go about it.

In Part 2 of this system I'll teach you techniques to lower your anxiety that work like magic. These techniques work at reducing your anxiety without distancing or distracting you from the situation you're in, which makes them perfect for exposure. You'll need to learn these anxiety-reducing techniques BEFORE you start your exposures.

So the right way to do exposures is to enter the situation that causes anxiety for you, do the anxiety reducing techniques I'll show you until your anxiety drops noticeably, then leave. You'll notice that over time your anxiety will diminish and, if you keep at it, it'll go away entirely. However, you MUST stay in the situation until you notice your anxiety levels drop.

# "What Happens If I Leave Early?"

**If you escape from the situation while anxiety is still rising, before it reaches its peak, then you will feel more anxiety the next time you try to face the situation.**

Why? Because if you escape from the situation to feel better temporarily, then you are conditioning your brain to associate running away from the situation with safety. Then if you try not to give in to the impulse to escape next time, you will find that your anxiety reaction is stronger. This is because you have unintentionally reinforced the link in your mind between the social situation that triggers your anxiety, and real danger.

Staying in exposure-type situations long enough for your anxiety levels to drop is what shows your brain that there's nothing to be afraid of. It rewires the emotional memory stored in your Amygdala because you leave the social situation feeling more relaxed, comfortable and at ease than when you entered it.

Exposure allows your body to get used to (habituate to) the anxiety and feel calmer the next time you enter an anxiety-causing situation. Your brain needs this firsthand evidence to unwire the anxiety.

**Remember that your brain wants proof, not promises.** You give it proof that there's no real danger through proper exposure.

# Imaginal Exposure

A lot of people ask me questions similar to: "I've heard I can lower my anxiety by using visualizations. Is that true?" The short answer is, yes, exposures through visualizations do have some effect in decreasing anxiety, and can be useful to some people, but only if done correctly.

> "Experimental and clinical psychologists have proved beyond a shadow of a doubt that the human nervous system cannot tell the difference between an 'actual' experience and one imagined vividly and in detail."
>
> **- Maxwell Maltz, M.D., F.I.C.S.**

Using imagination or visualization for exposure is called **imaginal exposure** in psychology. It is a valid method of exposure, but only when done correctly, and it's much less effective than exposure to real life situations.

It seems to me that many of the people who ask me about this type of exposure are trying to weasel their way out of the discomfort of facing their fears in real life. What they don't realize is that they should be feeling the same type of discomfort when they are visualizing, otherwise it does nothing.

The basic trick if you want to try visualization is to **make the situation in your head so real that you actually start to feel some anxiety**. If you don't start feeling somewhat anxious when you do the visualization, then it doesn't count as exposure, and your anxiety will stay the same.

Feel the anxiety (which means BE SOMEWHAT UNCOMFORTABLE) while doing this and stay in the situation mentally for long enough for your anxiety levels to drop noticeably. Even when you're doing visualizations, you'll have to use the anxiety-reducing techniques I'll show you in a few pages.

Make sure to imagine little details to really make the situation real in your mind. Set aside 5-10 minutes to do it properly.

The only real benefit imaginal exposure has is that you are more in control when facing the situation in the comfort of your home, and it can help to prepare you for real life exposures. IT CAN NOT AND WILL NOT CURE YOUR ANXIETY BY ITSELF. Remember that. You don't have to do visualizations (I almost never have), but it is 100% essential that you do real life exposures. That you face fears in real life.

# Mental Movies And Positive Expectancy

I'm going to take a bit of a detour for 2 minutes to make a related point.

If you think doing visualizations to overcome your SA is a bit weird, then keep in mind you're probably already doing visualizations without realizing it. The problem is, you're probably using them to hurt you instead of help you. People who are anxious or worried are constantly playing negative mental movies in their head.

**Many people who have SA will imagine themselves doing terribly in social situations, or they will replay an awkward situation in their head over and over again.** This is actually one of the worst things you could do to overcome your SA. The more you imagine negative outcomes happening to you, the less confident you will be in real life.

Think about it: if you always imagine yourself embarrassing or humiliating yourself, then what will you start to expect to happen in real life? You will expect to be embarrassed or humiliated. These negative expectations will make it so much harder for you to be confident or assertive.

**You should instead make it your goal to create positive expectations and assumptions for yourself.** People who are confident have the assumption that they will do well. This is why they are confident.

I'll talk about this more in a few chapters, but for now just become aware of the movies you play to yourself in your mind. If you imagine a situation going poorly, then you will be much more likely to avoid it. If you imagine a situation going well, or at least imagine yourself staying handling it well and staying relaxed, then you will be more likely to enter it with confidence.

Positive visualization is a something that almost all super-successful athletes do. Even actors, musicians and other performers do it. It's a secret to getting better at performing well under pressure.

If you don't feel like spending time every day imagining positive visualizations, then the least you could do is cut out the negative ones. Catch yourself when you are imagining or reliving a negative social experience, and cut it off. Stop sabotaging yourself.

What types of movies should you be playing in your mind to create that expectation of a positive outcome?

Now I'll get back to exposure

# What Is an Exposure Hierarchy?

An "exposure hierarchy" is the idea that you should expose yourself first to situations that only make you feel a little anxious (for example, making brief eye contact with a stranger). Then you work your way up to situations that make you feel more and more anxious (like approaching and starting a conversation with someone). You can almost think of a hierarchy as a ladder.

The benefit of this strategy is that it increases your chances of success. If you try to do something which scares you a lot before you can handle less intimidating situations, then you will probably fail. The failure may even cause you to stop trying to overcome your SA at all. So it's usually much better to desensitize in steps, where you move on to the next level when you first feel reasonably comfortable and relaxed in less intense situations.

If you ever feel you are slipping backwards, it could be because you are trying to run before you can walk. My best advice is to go one step at a time. Take things slowly and understand that unlearning old patterns of behavior takes time and effort. Even a small victory means you are not stuck, but need to keep working.

# A Hierarchy of Behavior

This step-by-step approach doesn't just apply to the types of situations you feel comfortable in. It can also apply to the <u>types of behaviors you feel comfortable doing</u>. Let me tell you what I mean...

Right now you may be a person who is quiet, timid, and keeps to himself or herself. From childhood, you've never been as confident as you'd like to be. So whenever you see someone who can be confident effortlessly, you assume they were "born that way" and you don't really believe that you can be like him or her. Well, I've got a secret for you: you CAN get better at social skills just like you can get better at any skill.

Have you ever joined a gym or taken a dance class? When you first walk in, you see all the advanced people, and it's maybe a little bit intimidating. They move about effortlessly, doing things you couldn't do if your life depended on it. But over time, your skill improves, until you eventually BECOME one of those people. This means slowly learning and developing new skills and expanding your comfort zone.

Overcoming SA is very similar to this. If you take simple consistent actions daily to continually expand your comfort zone, then in a relatively short time you will get better. You can become comfortable and at ease doing things which may now scare and confuse you. The key is to develop your level of social comfort and abilities progressively, which means to develop them gradually or in stages. The way forward is to slowly but steadily progress from the level you're at to the next level, to the next.

A typical sequence might look like this:

1. **Learning to relax around people.** Try taking your laptop to a café and getting used to being comfortable around people. (If your social anxiety is really bad, even this may take some time.)

2. **Learning to hold eye contact.** When you catch a stranger looking at you, hold it for a bit. Try not to be the first to look away. (Little warning: if you're a girl/woman and do this to a guy, he may take it as an invite to come talk to you.)

3. **Asking random people for directions.** Or saying hi to people on the street or giving them a compliment.. These are all good exercises in the beginning.

4. **Holding brief conversations.** With the cashier, or other people you usually avoid. For example, as you are paying, ask them about an item in the store.

5. **Being more assertive.** Looking on the internet and finding meet ups and clubs you can go to practice your new social skills. Go to these meet ups and introduce yourself to people.

6. **Being louder and more expressive.** Learning to relax and project your voice even when there's lots of people around.

7. **Getting comfortable with being the center of attention.** Staying relaxed even if several people are listening to what you're saying.

8. **Learning to be open with people to make them friends.** Instead of being secretive and withdrawn like most people with SA. (I'll talk more about this in the section called "Becoming Comfortable With Yourself")

9. **If you're a guy, approaching women you'd like to date** either in the day or at bars/clubs. (Albert Ellis, a world-famous psychologist, said he got over his shyness by spending a summer approaching girls in his local park and getting rejected over and over again.)

10. **Practicing public speaking** if that is a skill you want to have. Or taking improvisation theatre classes to become more spontaneous.

And so on...

The thing is, a lot of people think that confidence is something someone is born with. This is incorrect. It is a skill like anything else. A lot of people are lucky to grow up in situations which make it easy for them to build confidence. But even if you didn't develop it naturally as you were growing up, you can still become confident if you are willing to put in the effort.

# Creating Your Exposure Hierarchy

Here's how to create your own exposure hierarchy to overcome your SA.

1) **First you have to make a detailed list** of all situations in which you experience SA. Pick situations that come up fairly regularly, or at least ones that you could arrange to happen regularly. Be specific. Where is it and who is there? If you get stuck, try using some of the examples I just mentioned.

2) **Next, rank your feared situations.** Your list doesn't have to be perfect, you just need a general sense of which ones trigger low anxiety, which are medium, and which are high.

3) **The last step is to form a schedule** of when you'll be facing each situation, hopefully in rough order of difficulty. If you generally have a fairly busy life, then you may just need to learn to stop avoiding or partially avoiding the situations that come up. If you are alone at home all the time, you'll have to be more assertive about this and make the time to get out there and start conducting exposures.

If you want to use imaginal exposure or visualizations to "ease into" real life exposure, the best way is to do the imaginal exposure before the real life situation. So your exposure hierarchy would now look something like this:

- Imaginal exposure for situation #1
- Real life exposure for situation #1
- Imaginal exposure for situation #2
- Real life exposure for situation #2
- Imaginal exposure for situation #3
- Real life exposure for situation #3

# After An Exposure Session

Any time you face your fears instead of avoiding them, you've succeeded. Give yourself a pat on the back. Don't beat yourself up over minor screw ups. It doesn't matter if you did something wrong, or if the exposure didn't go well, or if you made a fool of yourself, or even if you think everyone is thinking terrible things about you. (Which is almost never true, by the way. People are way too focused on themselves to keep thinking about some screw up or mistake you made for more than a couple of minutes.)

The number one tip I can give you is to

## Focus on execution, not perfection.

What matters is that you keep getting new experiences that you can learn from and improve. Instead of beating yourself up, say to yourself "I'm taking steps to become better every day." Constant improvement towards a better you is what's important, not being perfect right now. As long as you did what you said you were going to do, you've succeeded.

If you have SA, then just the simple act of stepping outside of your comfort zone and doing something that scares you is going to be hard enough. Don't make it harder for yourself by placing unreasonable expectations for how well you "should" or "ought to" have performed.

If you managed to carry on a 5 minute conversation with someone you would have normally avoided, then you should feel great about yourself. Even if the conversation had an awkward moment or two, even if you didn't feel you were interesting enough, even if there's a million bad things you could focus on, make the choice to focus on the positive. You took a step in the right direction, so allow yourself to feel good about it.

By putting your focus on execution, you can also **get out of the trap many people of SA have of thinking there's some perfect thing to say or do**. It's a type of perfectionism. The reality is that social interaction is messy in a wonderful way. Conversations never sound like movie scripts. That's why you shouldn't place so much importance on perfection. To communicate effectively, you need to be able to adapt quickly to the social situation ... and you can always clarify something you said     but don't try to pre-rehearse the perfect thing to say beforehand.

# There Is No Failure, Only Feedback

**A great belief to live by is: there are no bad exposures, only learning experiences.** You WILL learn something every time you put yourself out there.

Even if you didn't think you did, your brain was still forming new connections automatically which will help you in future social situations. If you do well, your brain learns what you should do. If you do poorly, your brain learns what not to do. Your social skills are formed in a similar way that a skateboarder learns balance – through repetition and failure. So you will learn every time. The real evil in overcoming SA is not minor embarrassments or screw-ups, but avoidance.

**Even negative or humiliating experiences still work fine as proof.** Making a fool of yourself can actually teach you not to take yourself so seriously. When I realized this, it took a lot of pressure off of me to "perform well" in social situations. When you are first starting out overcoming your SA, make sure to take it easy on yourself. Don't beat yourself up or judge yourself too harshly.

# Rewards and Punishments

A good idea is to reward yourself in some way after you enter a challenging situation, whether or not it went well. It can be a candy bar or some other indulgence. A healthy one is better, but I'm trying to be realistic here. Why reward yourself? Because this type of positive reinforcement is often what is needed for some people with SA to push themselves into a situation that scares them.

On the other hand, some people respond better to possible punishment than potential reward. How can you use punishment to help you overcome SA? Every time you avoid a situation, do something that you don't want to. If you want to be extreme, then rip up a 20 dollar bill every time you know you have consciously avoided a situation because of your anxiety. That sounds crazy, but I've actually done it before, and it works. The point isn't to go into debt, but to associate more pain towards avoiding the anxiety than the pain of the anxiety itself. It may take a few experiments to find something that motivates you.

Why do I recommend using rewards and punishment for motivation? **It's because the actions people take are very often driven, not by their reason and logic, but by a simple need to gain pleasure or to avoid pain.** For example, you may logically know that the right thing to do is to face an anxious situations, but you may still not be able to get yourself to do it. The reason why you can't is because there is too much pain attached to facing the situation, and not enough pain to not facing it. If you can make avoidance painful for you in some way, by punishing yourself when you avoid anxiety, then your progress will be much faster. Make sure to play around with it and find a strategy that works for you.

The secret of success is learning how to use pain and pleasure instead of having pain and pleasure use you. If you do that, you're in control of your life. If you don't, life controls you.

-Tony Robbins

Lastly, make sure you actually carry out the consequences you say you will. That way you know that you're serious next time. If you don't actually do the reward/punishment, then it's not going to motivate you in the future. Actually carrying out the reward or punishment you said you would is the most important step. This is a very important principle whether you are parenting a child, coaching a team, or simply trying to hold yourself accountable.

# Progress and Motivation

The most important thing is to keep moving forward and getting used to more and more difficult situations. And the reason why I keep repeating this point over and over again is because that part is up to you. No one is going to accomplish this for you. If you need any more help, try getting a book on goal setting. I'm not going to try to motivate you, all I'll say is this...

**It's your life.** I've laid out a path that you can choose to walk down or not. I figure that the pain of years of loneliness and the potential of future friendships and romantic relationships is enough to motivate you to deal with the short term pain you'll encounter. It's what motivated me.

Don't be fooled: most people who try to overcome SA will fail at it. Why? Because most people are dabblers. They try something half-heartedly and then give up before they see any real change. It's just like losing weight – most people just jump on the latest diet and then don't stick to it long enough to see any real progress. They don't try to create a plan that they can realistically follow for months. Instead they get greedy for programs that promise results in days or a couple of weeks. When they quit, they immediately start looking for the next magic pill which promises to "melt fat from their body." This is a part of human nature.

Overcoming SA is simple. Especially when you have finished going through this system. You will know exactly what you need to do.

> But just because it's simple, doesn't mean it's easy.

Just like losing weight is simple: eat less, exercise more. But definitely not easy for most people.

The problem is not that both SA and being overweight are "not curable" as some claim. The real problem is that most people just don't have the willpower to stick at it and do the steps that are necessary to succeed.

In overcoming shyness or social anxiety, your progress will be the direct result of:

1) How often you enter anxiety-provoking situations.

2) How long these situations last on average.

A good number to shoot for is 4 times a week, at least 1-2 hours a day. Have small and achievable goals that are specific, so you know when you're making progress and when you need to push yourself or readjust your goals.

# Momentum – The Secret To Change

However, there is a secret to changing yourself which most people don't know. This secret is momentum. People who are stuck in a rut in life simply don't have any momentum to change their old habits.

**They are simply repeating the same behaviors from day to day on autopilot.** And because they have been stuck on this autopilot mode for so long they may even start to believe that change isn't possible for them. This is a lie. The truth is that anyone who has ever changed their life profoundly has always started out with something small.

For example, one of the best pieces of advice for someone trying to lose weight is to eat a healthy breakfast. It's a small change. The idea is not to change their diet and lifestyle around completely overnight. Just to eat one healthy meal at the start of the day.

Another example. People who are trying to become more financially responsible are often given the advice to cut down on a cup of coffee a day and put that money into a separate bank account. It's just one small daily change in behavior.

You may ask    What is the point of this type of advice? Nobody is going to lose a lot of weight just through changing one meal in their day. And nobody is suddenly going to get out of debt by saving a few dollars a day and not drinking coffee. So what's the point?

**The point is that this type of advice is just to get the person started building momentum to change their life.** Someone who starts making small but meaningful changes in their life will feel empowered to take control of their life in much bigger ways.

The person who eats a healthy breakfast is very likely to begin looking at more ways to eat healthy. They may even start exercising.

The person who cuts back on a cup of coffee a day will see how much money they are saving and they will start to notice many more ways they could save money. By not eating out as often, cutting back on expenses, and so on.

**In life, you build momentum through the decisions you make daily. Small changes lead to larger changes. Small stagnation leads to overall stagnation in your life, and you wind up repeating the same things day after day.**

As one famous quote goes

> "If you want something you've never had, you must be willing to do something you've never done."
>
> **– Thomas Jefferson**

So build that momentum to change through small decisions first. Break the avoidance habit. Build a new habit of facing your fears directly and challenging yourself to push into discomfort. Allow yourself to feel proud about the small victories. And you'll see yourself making progress quickly.

# Part 2
# Proven Anxiety Reducing Techniques

# Chapter 6
# Anxiety Technique #1: Diaphragmatic Breathing

Don't get intimidated by the long word "diaphragmatic." That's just the scientific name for the technique I'm going to teach you in this chapter.

**What "diaphragmatic breathing" really means is to breathe deeply using your belly.** This technique is probably the most well known technique for reducing anxiety. It's well known for a reason – it works.

As you'll find out in this chapter, diaphragmatic (or belly) breathing has excellent benefits for relaxation, lowering tension, decreasing stress and becoming calm. It's really one of the fundamental things EVERYONE should be doing in life.

Belly breathing has been proven to work through modern science. And even Buddha taught special breathing techniques thousands of years ago similar to this to increase mental health and lower stress!

What's even more interesting is that all babies do belly breathing naturally. But, for some reason, as people grow older and become more stressed and anxious about their life, many of them **forget how to breathe correctly**. They stop breathing through their belly (or diaphragm), and start using their chest to breathe. The truth is, most people don't know how to do something as basic as breathing correctly! This problem is compounded in people who have anxiety or nervousness issues.

"Slow, deep breathing is probably the single best anti-stress medicine we have. When you bring air down into the lower portion of the lungs, where oxygen exchange is most efficient, everything changes. Heart rate slows, blood pressure decreases, muscles relax, anxiety eases and the mind calms. Breathing this way also gives people a sense of control over their body and their emotions that is extremely therapeutic.

I have seen breath control alone achieve remarkable results: lowering blood pressure, ending heart arrhythmias, improving long-standing patterns of poor digestion, increasing blood circulation throughout the body, decreasing anxiety and allowing people to get off addictive anti-anxiety drugs and improving sleep and energy cycles.

**– James Gordon,**
Clinical Professor of Psychiatry,
Georgetown University School of Medicine

But before I can show you how belly breathing works, you first need to know a little about how the mind and body work together

# The Mind-Body Connection

One of the basic concepts of psychology is that the mind and body are interconnected. (They're actually the same thing, but let's just say they're interconnected.) The state your mind is in affects the state your body is in.

If you have SA, then you have probably experienced this first hand. When you are anxious, you may start sweating, shaking or blushing. That's your mind affecting your body.

What most people don't realize is that the opposite is also true. The state your body is in also affects the state your mind is in. If you start jumping up and down, then you won't be able to help but start _feeling_ more energetic on the inside. If you make your body relaxed, then your mind will also become more relaxed. Scientific studies have found that smiling makes you happier and confident postures make you feel more confident on the inside.[1] All this points to one life-changing fact

**If you change the state of your body, then your emotional and mental state will often follow.**

This principle is at the core of most of the techniques I'm about to show you.

# Shallow Breathing

The opposite of deep belly breathing is quick shallow breathing. Shallow breathing is caused by the fight or flight response I talked about before. In most animals, there's an automatic response when they are anxious, called the "fight or flight response". When this response becomes activated, then you start to experience physical symptoms of anxiety. You may start to sweat or shake, your muscles may tense up and your breathing will usually become shallower.

**Most people with SA start breathing faster and shallower when they become nervous or anxious.** This type of breathing causes you to become even more nervous, tense and "on edge" than you already are. And you probably haven't even noticed your breathing most of the time!

Shallow breathing not only fuels your anxiety, but it also causes you to have a weak, quivering voice and also...

# Cold hands!

The fact that their cold hands are caused by their anxiety often comes as a surprise to many people with SA. I remember my parents would always tell me to dress warmer and wear gloves when I was young because my hands were always cold. Happened every week in church at the time when everyone shakes hands. They would shake my

---

[1] For more on this, search Youtube for a speech called "Your Body Language Shapes Who You Are".

hand and become shocked at how cold it was even though we were in the warm church building.

So what does this mean if you often have cold hands and are reading this book? The fact is that your cold hands are not caused by not wearing enough clothes most of the time. **Your cold hands are usually caused by not enough blood circulation. And not enough blood circulation is caused by shallow breathing.**

When you breathe in a shallow way, your body doesn't get enough oxygen to recharge all of your blood cells completely. This means your body's ability to circulate blood is severely cut down. That's why your forearms may be warm, but your hands, especially your fingertips, are cold. Your blood simply doesn't have enough oxygen in it to go that far.

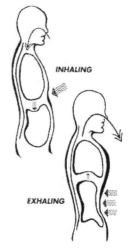

Now that you know some reasons why diaphragmatic breathing is so important, I'll get into the practical directions of how to do it.

# Diaphragmatic Breathing Step-By-Step:

Now I'm going to break down diaphragmatic breathing for you step-by-step and show you how to do it. Pay attention to these steps and practice them often, even on your own when you're not feeling anxious.

## 1. Breathe Using Your Belly, Not Your Chest

1) It may be easier to practice this lying down at first. As you're sitting in your chair or lying down, put one hand on top of your belly button and the other hand on your chest.

2) When you breathe in, you should feel your belly going out or expanding.

3) When you breathe out, you should feel your belly going in or contracting. Your chest and shoulders should barely move at all. Take a look at the diagram to see if you are doing this correctly.

4) **Use your hands to make sure you are doing this correctly.** Only the hand on your belly should move. The one on your chest should be mostly still. Your belly should be the part of your body that is expanding or contracting. Your shoulders should also not move up and down.

## 2. Take Long, Slow Breaths

If you want to help yourself relax, you must breathe slower. Breathing slower sends a signal to your brain that the situation is safe, and as a result, the anxiety you feel will usually go down.

**Breathe S-L-O-W-L-Y. Breathe in for at least 2-3 seconds. Most experts recommend you breathe out twice as long as you breathe in.**

When you are feeling anxious or nervous, you will probably not even realize just how fast you're breathing. So a good tip is to **count slowly as you are breathing** and keep track of how fast it is. This is especially important at the beginning when you aren't used to breathing slowly. It helps you stay aware of how fast you're breathing.

When you are breathing out, let the air escape naturally, don't try to force the air out of your lungs. Just relax your chest and belly and let the air come out on its own.

## 3. Breathe In Through Your Nose, And Out Through Your Nose Or Mouth

Breathe in through your nose most of the time. This may feel uncomfortable at first, like you can't get enough air, or like one of your nostrils is clogged, but you'll get used to it.

Someone who doesn't breathe through their nose is called a "mouth breather" by voice experts. Growing up, I always breathed through my mouth. I didn't realize I was breathing the wrong way until one day in high school I heard some kids having a conversation.

One of the kids had been sick for the past few days and he was saying, "Don't you hate it when you have a stuffy nose and you have to sleep using your mouth to breathe?" And the other kids all nodded and agreed. This was news to me. Up until that point I had almost always only breathed using my mouth, and I just assumed other people did the same.

It turn out that this isn't the case. Most people breathe in using their nose most of the time. Unless you are exercising, then you should try to do the same.

Breathing through your nose will make it much easier to breathe slowly and to do belly breathing. Mouth breathing when you're not exercising is a sign that you are anxious or stressed.

## 4. Breathe Out Quietly

Can you hear yourself breathing out as you practice? That's usually not a good sign. You should try to avoid making sound when you breathe out. Why? **It's because sound while breathing out is an indicator of tension in your chest and throat.** The tension is caused by anxiety (more on this in the next chapter   )

Remember to breathe out slowly and just let the air flow, don't force it. Relax your throat, chest and belly as you breathe and try to breathe more quietly.

## 5. Practice, Practice, Practice

When you're feeling anxious, you definitely want to focus on your breathing. Breath deeply, and slow it down. You'll find it's a great tool for calming yourself down as long as you stick to it. Don't just try it once for ten seconds and give up.

Belly breathing isn't just something you do when you're feeling anxious. It should be the way you breathe most of the time. This means you can practice diaphragmatic breathing almost anywhere.

Whenever you catch yourself using your chest to breathe, switch to breathing using your belly. If you keep consciously making yourself breathe in this new way, over time it will develop into a habit and you'll do it all the time without having to think about it.

Diaphragmatic breathing is one of the core techniques you need to master if you want to overcome anxiety in your life. So I encourage you to re-listen to this section, practice it in your spare time, and see the results in your life.

# Chapter 7
# Anxiety Technique #2: Muscle Relaxation

In this chapter I'll share with you a second technique that also works using the mind-body principle. This technique works by changing the state of your whole body, not just your breathing.

What is this technique? It's called muscle relaxation. In the next few pages I'll show you why you aren't doing it now, why you need to do it, and how to do it step by step.

By the end of this chapter, you'll realize one of the most important things you can do to reduce anxiety is to relax yourself as much as possible physically. It will make you calmer and less anxious in almost every situation you enter.  Once you learn to release the tension in your body, you'll find your inner nervousness and anxiety also becoming far less intense.

## Tension Is An Automatic Response

When your brain thinks there's danger, it automatically tenses your body up. Don't take my word for this – make sure you observe it in yourself.

**Next time you are feeling nervous or anxious in a social situation (your class, the store, answering the phone, etc.) try to keep part of your attention on your body.** Check to see which parts of your body tense up when you get anxious. Is it your face, jaw, neck, shoulders, chest, stomach, or a combination of these?

Make sure you pay close attention and try this exercise several times in several different situations – you may be so used to the feeling of being tense that it's hard for you to even recognize it anymore!

When I first began paying attention to the tension in my own body, it was a big breakthrough for me. I realized that muscular tension was basically a sign my body was giving me of when I was feeling anxious. And often if I hadn't been paying attention to my body, then I wouldn't have been able to relax in the situation and further unwire my anxiety.

I'll give you a specific example. I was a virgin even into my twenties because I was always quiet and shy around girls growing up. Later as I began overcoming my SA I started to get some success. But I still had almost no experience so, naturally, the first few times I was in bed with a girl, I was feeling very nervous and trying my best to hide it.

Here's where it gets interesting. I would be kissing a girl and then **she'd say something to me like "you're really stiff"**. This happened multiple times, with multiple girls, so it wasn't a one-time accident. The first couple times when they would say this, I wouldn't really know what they meant. But when I put attention onto my body, I soon realized they were right. "Wow! I really am tensed up!" Although I tried to LOOK relaxed on the outside, I wasn't really feeling relaxed on the inside.

Through trial and error, I realized that **consciously relaxing my muscles** and focusing on becoming less stiff actually worked wonders at making me FEEL more relaxed. It helped me immensely to unwire anxiety and become comfortable and relaxed even in intimate situations. Once I realized how powerful this technique was, I adapted it to decreasing anxiety and nervousness in many other areas of my life.

I want to explain a bit of the psychology behind this, because it's so fascinating and it will further hammer the point home of the importance of this technique.

# Body Armoring And Chronic Tension

People who suffer anxiety in many areas of their life – at home, school, work, and so on tend to develop chronic muscle tension in their body which is almost invisible to them.

This is something which truly surprised me when I first started doing work on body relaxation. I had never realized just how often my own shoulders and other muscles would be tense     even when I thought I was feeling "normal", not anxious!

A famous psychologist called Wilhelm Reich gave a name to this type of chronic tension related to fear. He called it "body armoring," which I think is a great name.

The idea behind body armoring is that people create tensions in their body in response to experiences, especially growing up. **When you repeat the same stressful experiences over and over again, then you start to develop habitual or chronic muscle tension in your body.**

The idea that nervousness and muscle tension are linked is nothing new. It's something that's been known and practiced in sports psychology for decades. One famous Olympic athlete coach said that if you ask an athlete to relax their neck and shoulders before their performance, they would usually drop them by about 3 inches. This is what I mean when I say that tension is an automatic response. These athletes didn't even know they were tense!

Everyone has some amount of unconscious muscle tension or body armoring, but people who have shyness or social anxiety are much more likely to have A LOT of tension. This is simply because their SA causes them to be stressed out more often in their daily life in more situations.

This tension is really a defense mechanism against what your body thinks is perceived danger. Your mind is ringing alarm bells, so your body tenses up to protect you.

# The Relaxation Response

There was a bestselling book published in 1975 called "The Relaxation Response" by a Harvard Psychologist called Dr. Herbert Benson. The book was groundbreaking because it called attention to the fact that stress and even blood pressure could be lowered simply by taking time every day to completely relax.

The book was also the first to talk about how the "fight or flight" response creates chronic lingering stress and muscle tension. Let me explain

Think of all of the times throughout your day when you become stressed, nervous or anxious – when making a phone call, talking to your boss, speaking up in class, going to the store, etc. Maybe you think that once you leave the stressful situation, you're back to "normal", right? Wrong.

**What Dr. Benson found was that the anxiety or "fight or flight" response still stays in your body long after the situation that caused your anxiety is gone.** It remains in your body as chronic muscle tension (body armoring) and also in the chemicals that were released in your body during the fight or flight response.

See, the fight or flight response basically "floods" your body and your mind with stress chemicals, which stay in your system for quite a while. These chemicals are very unhealthy to carry around for a long time and cause you to be "on edge". This means you need some way to regularly "flush" the stress chemicals and tension out of your body.

So how can you release this chronic tension and stress chemicals? In the book "The Relaxation Response," the author recommended a type of meditation which involves clearing the mind. I'll introduce you to mindfulness meditation later in the book. In this chapter I'll teach you a simpler muscle relaxation exercise which has a similar effect.

# Relaxation Unwires The "Fight or Flight" Response

Physical muscle relaxation works so well for anxiety because it deactivates the "fight or flight" response. When you make your body relaxed, you are sending your brain the message that everything is okay. **You are telling your brain: "I'm relaxed because there's nothing here to be afraid of - there's no danger."**

It goes back to the mind-body principle I talked about in the last chapter: the state your body is in affects the state your mind is in. Physical relaxation leads to less inner anxiety. It's that simple. Relaxation is one of the best "shortcuts" I know of to becoming a person who is comfortable and at ease in social situations.

# Other Benefits of Relaxation

Even beyond the anxiety and stress-releasing benefits, you'll find that **when you are totally relaxed, you have better body language automatically.** Many people with SA tense up when they are anxious so they have trouble walking and moving in a "natural" way. This causes all of their actions to look uncomfortable, stiff and self-conscious. Learning to relax your muscles properly goes a long way to fixing this problem.

Muscle relaxation also causes you to speak much, much better. Do you ever remember a time when you had to say something in front of many people and your voice sounded weird? I can definitely remember back when I had very bad SA whenever I was forced to talk in front of a lot of people (like reading something to the whole class) I would always be frustrated at how I sounded. Later I would always think "Why did my voice sound like that?" It would always sound much different and people would have a hard time hearing me and even understanding me.

But isn't it funny how when you are just talking to one person you know well, your voice always sounds much better? The reason why this happens is because it's **virtually impossible to talk well when your muscles are tensed up.** Especially when your jaw, throat, or chest muscles are tensed up. Your voice becomes weird and hard to hear instead of flowing and natural. When you tense up, you're basically cutting off the parts of your body which cause your voice to sound resonant and good. When you're tense, then it's like trying to speak clearly and loudly when someone is sitting on your chest!

The solution to this problem is to learn how to relax, even in situations when you feel anxiety. If you can learn to relax, then what you say will come out much, much better. Dr. James S. Greene, founder of the National Hospital for Speech Disorders in New York City, had a motto: <u>"When they can relax, they can talk."</u>

The first step in being able to relax on demand when you are feeling anxious is to practice at home. It's important for you to realize that if you have SA, then there's a good chance that you've forgotten completely how to relax!

If you are used to being tense, then being relaxed is what feels unnatural because you're not used to it. You actually have to re-learn how to be relaxed. Here's what you do:

# Muscle Relaxation Exercise

1) **Sit up comfortably** in your chair or lie down somewhere on your back.

2) **Go through your muscle groups one at a time.** Start at the top of your head and go down to your feet

3) **Tense, hold, and release each muscle group** as you go through them. First you have to tense it, hold it tense for a couple seconds, then let go of the tension and let it relax. After you tense, hold, and release each muscle group, you should become aware of where you were tensing your muscles. You should also feel more relaxed in that area of your body after you release.

4) **Go from the top of your body down to your feet:** forehead, face, jaw, neck, shoulders, arms, hands, back, chest, belly, buttocks, thighs, calves, feet and toes. It

doesn't have to be perfect, just try to hit as many major muscle groups as possible. Spend about five minutes on this. Take your time.

The reason why I get you to tense and hold each muscle group is because it makes it easier to release the tension. If you just try to relax, then it usually won't be as effective. You'll still be holding onto some tension unknowingly.

# Using Mental Imagery To Relax Deeper

The next step is to relax even deeper is by using mental imagery. The idea behind this is simple: If your mind is focused on something relaxing, then your muscles will automatically become less tense.

**Go back in your memory to some relaxing and pleasant scene from the past.** There is always some time in everyone's life when they felt relaxed, at ease, and at peace with the world. Maybe there was a time you were out by yourself in nature, or maybe you had a favorite secret place to go to when you were a kid.

If you can't think of one, then just imagine a scene you find relaxing. Maybe it's walking along a warm beach in the sand or maybe it's sitting at a peaceful lake in the mountains.

Imagine this scene and pay particular attention to the little details in the environment. What sounds were present? Did you hear leaves rustling through the grass nearby? How did the sand feel against your skin? Could you feel the warm, relaxing sun? Was there a breeze blowing? Were there gulls on the beach? The more of these little details in the environment you can remember, the more successful you will be.

**I recommend you practice the first muscle relaxation exercise every day.** Try doing it for five minutes right after you wake up. Put a note to remind yourself in front of your alarm. Daily practice will help to condition your body to be relaxed instead of tense. The more you do it, the easier it will become to enter that relaxed state again and again. (If you found the mental imagery exercise useful, then practice that as well.)

# Bringing Relaxation Into Daily Life

It's one thing to be relaxed in the comfort of your home while you're alone. It's a whole new challenge to make the decision to relax when alarm bells are going off inside your body. So how do you apply the techniques I've just shown you to actual, real life social situations?

1) **Diaphragmatic breathing** is the first step. You must remember to do this. Breathe in and expand your belly, breathe out slowly.

2) **Go through your muscles** and pay attention to where they are tensed up. People with SA often tense up their shoulders, belly and other parts of their body without realizing it. The biggest challenge is being aware of where your muscles are tense when you are in a tough social situation. In the beginning, try to remind yourself to keep some attention on your body before you enter an anxious social situation.

3) **Let go of the tension** wherever you feel it. It's easiest to do this as you breathe out. Simply exhale and relax the muscle. Try to make your body as loose and limp as possible.

4) **Try to "mentally remember" the relaxed feeling** you had at home. If you've been practicing, the feeling should be easy to replicate. See if you can feel any significant tension left in your muscles after you do this. If you can, release it by letting go.

At first you'll probably find that your muscles are tensed all of the time and you have to relax the tension every single time you check. But over time, you'll slowly find yourself becoming more and more physically relaxed. Eventually, you won't have to keep remembering to do it, you'll find yourself remaining relaxed in most social situations. To get to this point it will take some time though – maybe weeks or months to unwire your chronic muscle tension.

Remember that it took YEARS for you to become how you are now, so it's only reasonable to expect that it will take some time to un-condition your body's old habits. This doesn't mean you can't see quick results, though. It all depends on how diligent you are in remembering to use this technique in every possible situation you can.

# Chapter 8:
# Anxiety Technique #3:
# Acceptance

In this chapter I'll show you how to use a technique that will seem a little bit weird and unusual at first. The reason why it will seem weird is because **I'm going to tell you to do the OPPOSITE of what you probably usually do** now when you feel nervous or anxious. This technique is called Acceptance.

This is the shortest chapter in the system, but it's incredibly powerful. This technique is not just at the core of a couple of cutting-edge modern therapies (for example, Acceptance and Commitment Therapy), but it's also been tested to work for thousands of years in the techniques of Buddhism and other eastern spiritual practices. I've distilled it down to a few pages here. Make sure you listen to it several times to let the message really sink in.

# The Big Mistake: Trying to Hide Anxiety and Its Symptoms Or Force Them To Go Away

One of the things that makes social anxiety different from most other types of anxieties is the fact that a person with SA is afraid of the symptoms of the anxiety itself.

**In other words, when you feel anxious or nervous, you don't want anyone to know about it.** You want to hide the feeling or make it go away as fast as possible so people won't judge you for it.

This happens not just with the inner feelings, but also with the outer symptoms. You definitely don't want them to see you sweating, shaking or blushing. I remember I even used to be paranoid that other people could actually tell when my heartbeat was racing out of control. So you try to suppress and make the symptoms go away as fast as possible too.

You think this is helping you, but it's actually hurting you. The more you try to make people not see your anxiety or symptoms, the more pressure you put on yourself. And the more pressure you put on yourself, the more anxious you become. It's a vicious cycle. By putting pressure on yourself to NOT look anxious, you actually just make yourself more anxious, and you increase the symptoms of your anxiety.

# Other Ways of Struggling And Fighting With Anxiety:

Here are some more strategies <u>that don't work</u> when trying to overcome anxiety:

- **Insisting** you shouldn't be this way.
- **Fighting** feelings of anxiety using anger.
- **Complaining** about the fact that you have SA.
- Trying to argue that **"It's not FAIR"** that you have SA or that "You don't DESERVE" to have it.

# The Problem With Resisting

When you are experiencing a lot of fear and discomfort, it's only natural to want to try to get rid of these emotions in any way possible, at all costs. Unfortunately, using these types of strategies is <u>similar to throwing gasoline on a raging fire</u>.

Here's a quote by a famous author:

> "Whatever you fight, you strengthen, and what you resist, persists."
>
> **- Eckhart Tolle**

Which means is that resisting, fighting, battling, attacking, and getting aggressive with the fear or anxiety - just brings it on STRONGER. What you think should make the anxiety better is actually making it worse. **You can't fight a negative emotion with another negative emotion**, all you do is fall into a vicious cycle that gets very hard to break out of.

# The Chinese Finger Trap

Have you ever tried one of those Chinese finger traps? First you put two fingers into it at opposite ends. When you try to take them out again, you realize that you're stuck. The more you fight and try to pull your fingers out of the finger trap, the tighter it gets.

**The only way out is to relax and slowly pull your fingers out as you push the ends in.** Do you see how this relates to anxiety?

The more you fight it, the tighter its hold grows on you. That is why overcoming fear and anxiety is counterintuitive; that's why many people call it a paradox. If your fingers get stuck in a Chinese finger trap, the WORST thing you can do is to start pulling and struggling to get out of it. That's why most people get trapped in them. So, what do you do when anxiety tries to attack and hurt you?

# Play Dead

PLAY DEAD. Do not respond to it. Do not panic. Slow down. Take your time. Use the breathing technique you learned before. Focus on relaxing the tension in your muscles. Calm down, relax, cool it. Do not respond to negativity by reacting negatively.

You already know the more you fight, battle, struggle, and attack, the tighter the trap will get around you. Anxiety likes it when you fight back because then it has you trapped.  It won't go anywhere if you keep fighting.

**On the other hand, if you are calm and still, it becomes much easier to slip out of the trap unnoticed.** By not fighting anxiety, it will IGNORE you... you are not giving it any power to be able to harm you.

Don't get your fingers caught in the anxiety trap.  Take it easy, stay calm... then it will continue to have less and less power over you... and you will realize that YOU are the one who is in charge.

# Watch Your Feelings
# Without Involvement Or Judgement

When it comes to SA, almost all of the anxiety and fear you feel is false. It won't cause you any actual harm. Nobody has ever died from nervousness. All of your negative emotions are really just a chemical reaction in your body. That's all.

**Acceptance means simply watch your feelings without judging yourself based on your feelings.** So if you're feeling anxious, don't start worrying about "what this says about you personally." It's okay, it's just an automatic, conditioned response in your brain, and the best way to get over it is to not get involved with it.

View the nervousness or anxiety more like a scientist would view a chemical reaction happening from the outside. Cultivate the perspective of an observer watching your inner reactions with curiosity and always keep in mind

---

**1. Don't chase feelings, and don't run from feelings.**

and

**2. Whatever you're feeling, its okay.**

---

"Whenever fear comes to you, don't suppress it, don't repress it, don't avoid it, don't get occupied in something so that you can forget about it. No! When fear comes, watch it. Be face to face with it. Encounter it. Look deep into it. Gaze into the valley of fear.

Of course you will perspire, and you will tremble, and it will be like a death, and you will have to live it many times. But by and by, the more your eyes become clear, the more your awareness becomes alert, the more your focus is there on the fear, the fear will disappear. Like a mist."

**- Osho**

In reality, your anxiety or nervousness and the symptoms are not nearly as noticeable to other people as you think they are. And even if they were, they still wouldn't really care. Would you care if noticed someone looked nervous? You may say you would, but most people are too self-preoccupied to worry so much about others.

Here's one last point to tie up this chapter    When you feel like it's okay for other people to see you being nervous or anxious, then these feeling ironically tend to go away quicker. Why? It's because the root of social anxiety is trying to hide parts of yourself which you think are unacceptable to others.

So **by being willing to expose how you're feeling to other people, you will realize that it's not something you need to hide.** Through repeated exposure, you slowly take the shame out of your feelings and symptoms, and you break the vicious loop of social anxiety. It takes so much pressure off you when you don't feel like you have to always be putting on a performance around people, but that you can share your true self, regardless of whether you feel good or bad at the moment.

# Part 3 – Changing The Way You Think

> "Man's mind, stretched by a new idea, never goes back to its original dimensions."
>
> **- Oliver Wendell Holmes Jr.**

In this part of the system we're really gonna get serious. This is where the rubber meets the road.

Each chapter from now on is aimed to expand your mind and update your inner software to make you go from shy or socially anxious to confident in as little time as possible. You'll understand your past behavior and personality in crystal clear detail in ways you can't yet imagine. You'll see the mistakes you were making in the past that were keeping you stuck – and how to avoid them.

You'll get specific directions to overcome issues like insecurity about your appearance, self-consciousness, and overthinking what to say. You'll learn how to overcome toxic shame, become spontaneous in social situations, and draw friends towards you magnetically.

Let's get started.

# Chapter 9
# Value And The Social Hierarchy

Do you ever feel like some people you try to talk to automatically brush you off? They don't let you talk, and don't really listen to what you have to say?

And then you see these exact same people giving their full attention to other people, who are seen as being popular?

**Doesn't that just piss you off?** I remember that used to happen to me all the time. It seemed like everybody cared about themselves and other social people, but nobody seemed to care what I had to say, even if I tried to be more outgoing. Even if what I said was funny or interesting, while other people were just saying dumb, obvious things.

It got to the point where sometimes I got the feeling I was annoying people just for talking to them. Why did most people never make an effort to come start a conversation or be friends with me? Why did they always go talk to other people instead? Why was I almost never invited out? Was it because I was shy? Or something else?

If you've ever wanted to know the hard-core psychological science behind what makes some people magnets for friends and attention, and others desperate for any social contact, then what you are about to read will blow your mind.

## The Concept of Value/Status

Have you ever seen a totem pole?

It's a tree trunk carved to show a series of heads, one on top of the other. There's a picture of a totem pole on the right so you get the idea.

Social groups work the same way as a totem pole in a lot of ways. In every social group, there is usually a hierarchy from the highest to lowest member of the group. It's like a scale from the most important to least important person. Different people have a different value or status in the group and they are treated differently based on their value.

**Scientists who study animal groups often call this a dominance hierarchy.** In many species of animals, this dominance hierarchy is very obvious. For example, groups of chickens establish a hierarchy of who gets to eat and mate first by pecking each other. By pecking each other, the chickens figure out who is the "top chicken," the "bottom chicken" and where all the rest fit in between.

In other species of animals, like humans, the social hierarchy is usually not so obvious. It's definitely still there, but you're only gonna see it if you know what signs to look for. The social hierarchy is more like an undercurrent that controls much of people's behavior below the surface (including your own behavior).

For example, at work, do you treat your boss differently than your co-workers? Of course you do, because he is "higher up the food chain", so to speak. The boss has higher social value than the employees in the workplace. You are probably more careful not to offend him or her and may even have difficulty carrying a conversation.

It's the same with the relationship between the teacher and student. Or police officer and citizen. The person put into a position of authority is by default the higher value person.

**And think about how you treat someone you are very attracted to** compared to someone you aren't. Are you automatically anxious around them? Do you have trouble making eye contact? Are you constantly imagining future conversations or replaying small interactions that happened in the past? All of these behaviors are symptoms of placing that person above you, and feeling inferior to them by comparison because of their superficial attractiveness.

So far I've given you some very obvious examples of value. But even in casual social situations, there's usually still a hierarchy. It's just invisible to most people. The goal of this chapter is to make the social order or hierarchy visible to you.

# How Social Value Causes Social Anxiety & Shyness

Right now you may be thinking "This is all very interesting, but how does it relate to my SA?"

I'll explain it to you. You already know that SA is fear of disapproval. What you may not know is that <u>you only really fear the disapproval of people you think are higher value or superior than you.</u>

Think about this long and hard, because it's a crucially important point. You only care about the disapproval of people who you think have a "higher value" than you do.

**We interact with people differently based on how valuable we see them.** If you place a lot of value or importance on someone, then you are going to act a lot more inhibited and anxious around them then someone you don't care so much about.

If you don't believe me that you treat different people differently based on how much you value them, then try this exercise: go out and ask two strangers for the time. One is a ten year old child, the other is someone your own age you find attractive. What do you think would happen? You probably wouldn't even be able to walk up to the attractive person because you care so much more about what they think of you. And it's because of how you value them.

**In every interaction between two people, one person is higher value/status.** (I'm using the words value and status interchangeably, by the way.) He or she may be better-connected socially, more dominant, a better leader, more popular with everyone, or just more confident and comfortable with themselves. For girls, good looks also are a large factor. So one person is always "cooler".

If you want to know whether you believe somebody is higher value than you, then a quick question you can ask yourself is:

> ## Who do you view as important enough to
>
> ## 1) Affect you emotionally and
>
> ## 2) Cause you to change your behavior?

From now on, notice when your anxiety or shyness is being triggered by being intimidated by someone's social value.

**For example:**

- **Can you can easily talk to people who are seen as being "uncool",** but struggle to say the right thing when talking to someone popular? (By the way, popular is just the word I'm using because it's easily understandable. You can substitute many traits, like how aggressive, assertive, confident well-connected or intelligent the other person is.)

- **Have you ever wanted to be seen with someone** because you thought other people would see you with him/her and think you were a cooler person because of it? This may be as subtle as trying to stand close to the "cool" person.

- **When you walk past people on the street,** are you more anxious when you are walking past an elderly couple or someone attractive around your own age? I'm guessing it's the latter.

- **Do you ever want to show someone popular your better qualities,** like being much more energetic and social when they are around, name-dropping, or mentioning things (material possessions, interesting life events, etc.) you hope will impress them?

- **Do you get a lot more secretive and insecure about your life** when talking to certain people? It's because you care more about what they think of you.

- Do you become very self conscious around certain people? For example, do you constantly check your clothing and appearance around someone you find attractive? Pay attention to when you look down at your clothes or feel an urge to look in a mirror.

- Do you ever pretend to be more interested in certain things (sports, hobbies, pop culture that you wouldn't usually be interested in) just to try to fit in with someone?
- Do you instantly become more quiet, shy and inhibited when certain people walk into the room?

**If you do any of these things, don't worry, you aren't alone.** The important thing to notice is that you are never actually trying to treat everyone differently. It just happens. Everyone has this type of automatic system of valuing people. It controls how they act around who.

But here's a warning: now that you understand that people pay more attention to people of higher value, and almost ignore people who are lower value, you're going to see this happening everywhere.

Don't say I didn't warn you.

# Value, Self-Esteem and Anxiety

Okay, so from now on notice how your shyness and anxiety is much greater whenever you are talking to someone who has "high value". These are the people you consider superior to you subconsciously. You perceive their worth to be greater than yours, so you get nervous around them. You don't feel entitled to express yourself confidently around them. In a way, you feel intimidated.

On the other hand, when you are talking to someone you don't think is superior to you, then you are naturally going to be much more comfortable, relaxed and free to express your personality. When you feel like someone is "on your level" or even "less cool" than you, then you will usually feel little or no anxiety around them.

Around people you think are higher value than you, you may become awkward and struggle with not running out of things to say. On the other hand, around people who you think are lower value than you, you aren't even worried about it. The possibility of running out of things to say doesn't even cross your mind, because you're simply comfortable around them.

So let me repeat this, because this is probably the most important point in this chapter

**When you don't feel inadequate compared to the person you are talking to, your confidence and social skills come easily and naturally.** It's only when you are intimidated by someone else or feel inferior to a group of people that your mind goes blank and you start acting shy.

And if this is true, then one of the best ways to decrease your anxiety and increase your social skills is to raise your perception of your own value or worth. This is also called your self-esteem.

> "Self-esteem is a term used to reflect a person's overall evaluation or appraisal of his or her own worth."
>
> **- Wikipedia.org**

I'll show you how you can improve your self-esteem, or perception of your own value, in the next chapter. For now just remember how it fits into anxiety and value. Keep in mind that the word "self esteem" is used by a lot of people in a lot of different ways. It has many definitions. A lot of self help writers talk about self-esteem in a wishy-washy feel-good type of way. That's not how I'm going to talk about it. When I talk about self-esteem, I'm referring to something very real, tangible and specific – your perception of your own worth. Your self-esteem is very real because it can be seen through observing your outer behavior.

# What Makes You See Someone As Valuable?

We will talk much more about this in the next chapter, but I'll cover it briefly here. What you may be thinking about right now is: what makes someone high value or superior in the first place? I'll try to answer that quickly here.

The first thing to understand is that value is all in your mind. In reality, there are no "superior" or "inferior" people. The only reason why you see some people as more valuable than you is because you have some <u>rules in your mind</u> that determine whether someone is valuable to you or not. If someone passes all these rules and criteria you have, then you see them as valuable.

So let's talk about what some of these rules could be.

**Ask yourself:**

- Does someone's confidence, decisiveness, assertiveness or aggressiveness often intimidate me? (Often just the fact that someone SPEAKS LOUDLY is enough to make others see them as being important.)
- If I see someone as having a lot more friends and social connections than me, do I feel inferior to them? If you see a lot of people commenting on their facebook, for example, do you immediately see them differently?
- If someone is very physically attractive and/or wears the most stylish clothes, do I act differently around them? (Pay special attention to how differently you treat women who are below-average looking and women who are drop-dead gorgeous. This happens with men too, but not as much. Men are valued more on their confidence, which is a behavioral indicator of status. )
- Do I have trouble speaking to people in positions of authority? Teachers, bosses, job interviewers, etc.
- Am I more anxious around people my own age, the very old, or the very young? (It's usually people your own age or somewhat older people that are most

intimidating. Very old people and very young people are usually easier to be relaxed around.)

And when you're asking yourself these questions, it's important to look at your actions and behavior. **Your behaviors will reveal your unconscious beliefs to you.** Pay attention to how your level of confidence or nervousness changes based on the situation and the people in it. This can give you an indicator of how you value yourself compared to other people, and where you feel inferior.

**People who have SA tend to over-value other people and place them on a pedestal.** I remember back when I had really bad SA I would tend to over-value almost everyone else. I would think of pretty much everybody as being "above me". When you have low self esteem, you often see everyone else as being really interesting, likeable, popular, etc   even if it's just an average person.

# What Makes You See Yourself As Being Low Value Or Inadequate?

Along with over-valuing other people, you probably also tend to under-value yourself. The two go hand-in-hand.

If you have some rules in your mind that cause you to see some people as being superior to you, then you must also have some rules that cause you to see yourself as being inferior.

Part of this is caused by the toxic shame we talked about earlier, another part of it could have been learned or picked up over time from critical parents, the superficial media, or simply a tendency of being overly critical and perfectionistic towards yourself.

**It's also a question of selective focus.** Scientists have found that people who have shyness or social anxiety tend to focus on negative feedback much more than positive feedback. So, for example, you do a speech, and you notice the one person not paying attention, rather than everyone else paying attention (and the five people who told you "Good job!" after).

Or you focus and replay an awkward moment over and over again, instead of remembering the good conversations you've had that day. When you focus on the negative like this, your mind slowly begins to form a negative, distorted picture of yourself. And this picture leads to inferiority.

Regardless of how you got to where you are now, here's the thing you need to understand

**If you have low self-esteem, it means that you do not think you meet other people's rules for being a valuable person.** You believe you can see yourself through other people's eyes, and you judge yourself by what you imagine other people's standards to be.

# Becoming Invested In Yourself

Have you ever had someone give you the advice that you need to just "stop caring what people think of you"? Although they were technically correct, their advice was too generic.

Here's a better way to think of this:

> **You overcome SA by putting your own opinion of yourself over other people's opinion of you.**

You care about other people's opinion of you more than your own opinion of yourself. And this causes you to become very emotionally invested in how they see you. This is why you get nervous or anxious, especially around people you place a high value on.

So right now you unconsciously value other people too much and you value yourself too little. And this is destroying your confidence. As you'll discover in the next chapter, the "rules" in your head that cause you to see yourself as inferior to certain people are false and irrational, and they can be reprogrammed.

The key is to start judging yourself by your own standards, instead of other people's. And make yourself live up to your standards so that you "become a hero in your own mind." When you raise your perception of your own value, and stop placing other people above you, then it becomes easy to be confident and natural in almost any social situation.

# Chapter 10
# From Shame To Confidence: Inferiority and Assumptions

## What's Your "Secret Reason?"

One thing that I have noticed time and time again when it comes to people who are unsuccessful in some area, is that almost all of them have a "secret reason" to justify their failure.

When it comes to your SA and lack of social life, what is your "secret reason" for not being able to do what other people can do?

Often it is insecurity about your appearance, many people with SA have some serious body image problems. You may feel other people can't or won't accept you for how you look. Short, tall, bald, hairy, skinny, fat, bad teeth, large nose, foreign accent, ugly, etc.

Other times the "secret reason" is based on your upbringing. Maybe you blame your current condition on how your parents brought you up. If your parents were very introverted and didn't have much of a social life, then you say you "learnt it from them." If your parents were very loud and outgoing, then you may say "their outgoing nature caused me to retreat and become introverted."

**Ask yourself: "What is my secret reason?"** Dig deep, find out what it is. Maybe you have more than one. Maybe you have several. What story you use in your mind to justify your failures up until now?

At this point in my career of helping people overcome their shyness and social anxiety, I think I've heard every possible secret reason that exists. Of course I've heard the ones about having a bad childhood and a bad appearance, but I've also heard some more bizarre ones.

I had one guy tell me: "I'm so good looking that people are intimidated. That's why I can't have relationships." And he wasn't kidding or trying to be arrogant. This is something he actually believed to the core. He believed the reason people didn't like him was because they were either secretly jealous or intimidated.

I've had some people tell me that they "turned out this way" because their parents never took an interest in developing their social life. I've had other people tell me that their parents caused their SA because they encouraged them to participate in sports at a young age, which made their problems much worse.

Sometimes the "secret excuse" was a traumatizing childhood event, other times it was being too sheltered and protected in childhood.

And here's one that I have to mention purely because it's so common. Many men feel inadequate around women based on feeling like they have too small sex organs, and many woman think their sex organs are too large! Some feel they have too low sex drive, others feel their sex drive is too high.

Are you starting to see a pattern here? The range of "secret excuses" people have is gigantic, and often one person's excuse is the exact opposite of someone else's.

With this in mind, I want you to start to open your mind to the possibility, just the slight possibility, that **your "secret excuse" is not the cause of your social problems, but only a justification for them.**

# Your Image of Your Self

What really put me onto to trail of the "secret reason" was a book called "Psycho-Cybernetics," written by a plastic surgeon called Dr. Maxwell Maltz.

What Dr. Maltz noticed was that he had two types of patients who came in for plastic surgery. The first type of patient would receive plastic surgery, and many of their inner psychological problems would be solved. They would no longer feel inferior, inadequate, or embarrassed because of their appearance. This makes sense, doesn't it? If you get rid of the cause of embarrassment, then what is there left to be embarrassed about?

But then there was a second type of patient. Even when the "defect" was fixed, many patients still had the same psychological problems. They still felt the same low self worth they always had. The same sense of embarrassment about themselves remained even though they had "fixed" the cause!

**The outer scars were healed, yet the inner scars remained the same.** What did this mean?

What Dr. Maltz discovered was that everyone not only has an outer image or appearance, they also have an inner image. Everyone has a self-image, it's a picture in your mind of who you think you are. It's the collection of beliefs you have about yourself and what you think you are capable of. Even though plastic surgery had gotten rid of the patients' "secret reason", their self-image remained the same.

"The self-image controls what you can and cannot accomplish, what is difficult or easy for you, even how others respond to you just as certainly and scientifically as a thermostat controls the temperature in your home. Specifically, all your actions, feelings, behavior, even your abilities, are always consistent with this self-image. Note the word: always. In short, you will "act like" the sort of person you conceive yourself to be."

- Maxwell Maltz, M.D., F.I.C.S.

Why is it that when you try to act more confident and social, it always feels like you have to force it? Like you're putting on an act? It's because you are trying to change your outer behavior without changing your self-image and inner beliefs. That's why you can "fake" confidence for maybe a couple of minutes, hours or days, but then you go right back to being shy and introverted.

When you try to "act" confident, it's like a fish that's trying to swim upstream. It can do it for a bit, but eventually the stream overpowers it and it is swimming in the direction it always has. The stream is like your self-image, and it is always bringing you back to acting in ways that fit your self-image. If your self-image says you are low value and inferior to other people, then you will find it difficult to act in ways that contradict your inferiority. At least, not for long.

For example, an overweight person can lose weight through sheer willpower, but if they see themselves as a "fat person", then they will feel a gravitational pull to become the person they conceive themselves to be. This is why many overweight people seem to be constantly losing a bit of weight, then going back to their old habits, and gaining it all back the next month.

# Your Self-Image Forms Through Early Childhood Experiences

Okay, so where do you get these beliefs into your self-image that "you are inferior"? You don't believe something ever unless you think there are good reasons to believe it is true.

**This is where we come back to toxic shame.** In case you don't remember, toxic shame is a belief that you as a person are not lovable or acceptable just as you are.

This belief often forms through you not getting unconditional approval and acceptance at a stage of life when you needed it – early childhood. Usually, it's a result of accidental experiences of parental neglect or abandonment, but it can also be caused by bullying, rejection or disapproval from other authority figures.

## Here Are Some Signs of Toxic Shame

- You feel like you need to hide certain parts of your life, personality, or interests from others.
- You don't feel like people could accept you just as you are.

- You are extremely uncomfortable with closeness or intimacy with other people, which causes you to withdraw and isolate yourself from others.
- You feel inadequate, not good enough, unworthy of love.
- You're usually depressed and focused on all of the parts of you which are "not good enough."

In addition, toxic shame can make you feel low value/status in almost all situations. This goes back to the last chapter. While some people get intimidated when talking to someone very attractive, or famous, or in a position of authority, people who have severe social anxiety get intimidated by almost everyone. In other words, they constantly feel like they are low value compared to almost everyone they talk to. They feel chronically low status.

(**Note:** Sometimes feelings of inferiority are not originally caused by toxic shame, but simply by bad habits of thinking – such as comparison. I'll talk more about this in the next chapter.)

# Your Beliefs Are Reinforced Daily

Much of your self image and beliefs were formed accidentally during your childhood. But the way your self-image reinforces itself and becomes stronger is through the experiences you have on a daily basis.

**If you have lots of experiences that show you that you are inferior, then that's what you are going to believe.** If nobody ever invites you out or makes an effort to get to know you, then you will feel even more inferior than you already do. If you are the girl who didn't get asked to dance at the dance, then you will definitely believe you are less desirable than the other girls.

Your beliefs or image about yourself develop through your experiences, and what you believe your experiences say about you. But here's where it gets interesting

# Your Self-Image Is a Self-Fulfilling Prophecy

In the quote above, Dr. Maltz said "[...]all your actions, feelings, behavior, even your abilities, are always consistent with this self-image?" This is the key.

If you believe deep down that you are low value and inferior, then you will behave in ways that communicate to people that you believe you are inferior. You will be much less confident around them, unable to hold eye contact or your voice will become quieter and less expressive. You may feel like you lose your personality around people you don't now well. Or you may just try too hard to seek their approval.

When you act as though you are inferior, the other person sees this and has no choice but to believe you. If YOU think you are inferior, then you must be. **After all, who knows you better than you know yourself?** He will then treat you as if you are inferior to him. When you see this you will gain further "evidence" of your inferiority, not realizing that you are the source of this "evidence". Your beliefs are a self-fulfilling prophecy.

Here's a specific example from the plastic surgeon's book:

> "A young girl who has an image of herself as the sort of person nobody likes will indeed find that she is avoided at the school dance. She literally invites rejection. Her woe-begone expression, her hang-dog manner, her over-anxiousness to please, or perhaps her unconscious hostility towards those she anticipates will affront her-- all act to drive away those whom she would attract. Her actual experiences tend to 'prove' her self-image is correct."
>
> **- Maxwell Maltz, M.D., F.I.C.S.**

**Your experiences tend to reflect your self-image back to you.** Because of this objective "proof" it very seldom occurs to people that their trouble lies in their self-image or their own evaluation of themselves. Tell the girl at the dance that she only "thinks" she is unattractive and she will question your sanity. If boys do not ask her to dance, then she must be unattractive! The evidence proves it.

# The Truth About Your "Secret Reason"

So what am I saying here? I am saying that whatever your "secret reason" is, it is not true! Your background, your looks, any physical "defects", your life situation, your upbringing -- all of these do not matter when it comes to achieving social success! They may have contributed to making you feel inferior or inadequate up until now, but they do not have to control your future. Any "secret reason" you have of why you can't be as outgoing and social as other people must be dropped.

It's not your looks or life situation themselves, but your thoughts about them that hold you back. I know this may sound hard to believe at first, but think about it. **Haven't you ever seen anyone with the exact same "problem" you have still be able to be confident and outgoing?**

Maybe you feel insecure because you are overweight or unattractive -- there are plenty of people out there who are overweight and not good looking, yet they are still able to have self esteem that allows them to be confident and express themselves. They may be overweight, but they don't see themselves as inferior or a failure because of it.

Maybe you feel depressed and miserable because of your upbringing, your parents were never very social so you "learned it from them." Or maybe you remember some embarrassing event from your past that started your social anxiety.

I'm not saying that these aren't all perfectly valid reasons for someone to develop social anxiety or an inferiority complex, but here's the cold, harsh truth:

Every single excuse ever made for why someone cannot be confident, or have a social life and friends ... has been met and conquered by people with more flaws, less brainpower, less money, less skill and less resources than you. There are people out there who have the same source of inferiority or shame you do who are still socially successful in spite of it.

They have the same excuse or reason you do, but they do not attach a feeling of inferiority or shame onto it. They do not feel bad about not looking like a model, or not having the life of a rockstar.

This doesn't mean you have to blame your social anxiety on yourself, but you do have to acknowledge the fact that you are able to respond once you decide to do something about it.

If you don't believe me, then go and watch this video:

http://www.youtube.com/watch?v=H8ZuKF3dxCY

It's a video about a guy who was born with no arms and no legs, yet he doesn't let that hold him back. Notice how he is still able to be confident and doesn't think he is inferior in any way?

> "Freedom is what you do with what's been done to you."
>
> - Sartre

# Confidence is an Assumption of Acceptance

What is confidence?

Before I can answer that question, let's first have a clear idea of what confident people do.

- Confident people enter situations headfirst. For example, if they want to talk to someone, they walk right up and introduce themselves.

- Confident people speak their mind. They aren't overly concerned with whether they say something offensive to others.

I could list many more examples, but these two should be enough. Try to think of confident people you know and see how they act. Imagine how they would call someone on the phone or introduce themselves to someone new or maybe walk into a group and join a conversation.

As you imagine these people, think about this carefully: What makes their behavior "confident"? In other words, what is the message communicated by their actions that makes them be seen as "confident" by other people? Well, after studying this area for a long time I think I have finally nailed down what confidence truly is at the core

**I believe that behind every confident behavior is an assumption of acceptance.** When someone is confident, they assume that other people will react positively to them. This is why they can step into new social situations headfirst and talk to new people without fear. They have a belief that they will be accepted. The possibility of rejection or embarrassment barely even registers to them.

This belief that they will be accepted tends to become true because people react well to their confidence. It's a self-fulfilling prophecy. Here's a way you can test this out in real life:

**Try approaching someone new with the same energy as you would approach an old friend.** When I say energy, I mean the warmth and welcoming tone to your voice and body language. You really need to try this experiment out in real life to see the power of it. When you go to talk to an old friend, your voice and body language unconsciously communicate an assumption that the person will be friendly to you right away.

And if you can mimic this assumption of acceptance and friendliness when talking to someone new, then the majority of the time they will be very friendly. They will usually mirror your friendliness back to you.

**People take their cues for how to treat you based on your behavior.** You are the source of how people treat you. If you want people to like you, then you must believe yourself to be a likeable person. And you communicate this belief through your assumptions and they way your assumptions control the way you act.

# Anxiety Is An Assumption of Rejection

On the other hand, let's look at the behavior of someone with SA:

- Afraid of approaching people and tries to avoid it. When you see someone you want to go talk to, you probably wait and try to think of "the right thing to say".

- Afraid to just speak your mind. Everything has to be carefully filtered so you don't "look dumb" and make a bad impression.

- Afraid to pick up the phone, especially not knowing who it could be. People with more severe anxiety may be afraid of even buying something at the store or ordering a sandwich.

- **You play it safe. You act in the ways that <u>you hope</u> will get you acceptance from the majority of people.** If you stay quiet, then there's very little risk that you're going to offend anyone. And you only feel free to express yourself or "open up" when there is no chance that the other person will reject you -- a family member or close friend.

- You worry about what to say in conversations and are anxious about hiding your perceived flaws from other people. If you do talk to someone new, you are shy and timid because you're afraid, which makes the situation awkward.

What do these behaviors have in common? **"Behind" shyness or social anxiety is an <u>assumption</u> of rejection or disapproval.** Someone who is avoidant, afraid or hesitant of social situations is revealing their belief that they think they are likely to be rejected. They assume they are not going to be liked.

Why? Because of either toxic shame created in childhood or feelings of inferiority created through bad thinking habits, or a combination of the two.

# The Approval and Inferiority Contradiction

Do you see how your beliefs about yourself create your shyness and anxiety? Think about this carefully

**Shame and inferiority literally create your anxiety** most of the time because, when you think there's something wrong with you, you assume other people are likely to reject you. This creates an irrational fear of disapproval.

Do you remember back to the beginning of this system when I told you that SA was rooted in a fear of disapproval? You are socially anxious because deep in your mind you have a core belief that says: "I must be liked. I must be approved of    or else something terrible will happen."

Okay, now let's bring back the "secret reason." You think some part of you is repulsive or unacceptable in some way    yet you want to avoid all disapproval from others. Do you see the contradiction here? You need and demand approval, while at the same time feeling it is impossible for other people to approve of the "real" you because of some defect. This is a ridiculous combination, and it leads to much of your suffering.

Your negative beliefs about yourself cause the assumption of rejection, and therefore the anxiety, nervousness, and lack of confidence you feel.

If you assumed people would accept you, then your anxiety and shyness would be much lower. And since you would be more relaxed    people would ironically be much more likely to like you.

So how do you overcome the toxic shame and inferiority which causes SA and leads to beliefs of being low value? The answer starts on the next page…

# Chapter 11
# From Comparison To Unconditional Self Acceptance

This is going to be a dense chapter, but it's one of the most important ones in this system. I'm about to set up the foundation for your new inner software. The software that will, over time, dissolve your anxiety and shyness in social situations. I'm going to repeat a few of the points in this chapter a few times in different ways to really hammer it in. This repetition is intentional.

## The Comparison Trap

Maybe you have heard before how inferiority is the result of comparing yourself to others. If you compare yourself to others and come up short, then you feel a sense of shame about yourself. It's easy enough for others to tell you to "stop comparing yourself to people," but it's much more difficult to live that philosophy.

In the first place, you have been <u>conditioned</u> since childhood to achieve.

**The importance placed in modern society on proving one's worth, on material success, on status, on measurable achievement** is acutely felt by children. To be loved, accepted, and valued, they must produce the desirable responses. People are recognized on the basis of what they have produced -- not on who they are.

You know there's a problem when the values of society put such an overemphasis on competition and individual achievement. I remember my parents would always treat me better if I brought home good grades. This makes sense on the surface -- all parents want only the best for their kids.

Unfortunately, they were unintentionally conditioning me to believe that performing well was the way to get love and approval. Maybe your parents showed you more affection when you performed well in sports, dance, school, work, or some other area. And when you didn't live up to their expectations you wouldn't get the same amount of approval.

This type of early childhood conditioning is part what makes your self esteem and confidence bad to this day. You may have deep-seated beliefs that you are not a worthwhile person unless you achieve, unless you are the best, unless you live up to other people's expectations when it comes to your social life, relationships, and financial situation. When you equate what you do with who you are, you feel inferior or superior to others.

# Beauty and Self Esteem

Many people who have SA feel insecure about their appearance. In our culture, beauty is considered the prime measurement of human worth. All you have to do is turn on the TV or walk down a magazine aisle to see it. People are being conditioned and brainwashed into believing that the more good looking someone is, the more valuable they are. This is crazy if you think about it, it's literally insane!

The vast majority of movies, advertisements, TV shows and magazines out there try to make you buy into their philosophy. The philosophy of "Look like this or you're ugly. Buy our product to make yourself more valuable." You have to reject their message and not buy into it, because if you buy into the superficial values of the media, then you will never measure up. You could be a doctor who's saved thousands of lives, but you'll still feel inferior to someone who happened to be born good looking by accident!

One of the biggest example of this are the emails I receive from shy guys who tell me that they freeze up around women they find very attractive. They have been conditioned to place so much value on a woman's looks that it completely takes over them when they see a pretty girl. Meanwhile, they usually have little difficulty talking to a woman who is considered average or unattractive.

**Ask yourself: Do people really deserve to be valued and put on a pedestal based on their <u>luck</u> in getting the right genes?** Am I acting rationally when I am intimidated by someone like an attractive woman for no reason, or have I been unconsciously conditioned by the media to value looks over virtually everything else?

Whether you feel inferior based on your looks, upbringing, race, or current level of success socially, financially or relationship-wise, all feelings of inferiority come down to the same thing. You judge and measure yourself, not by your own standard, but against someone else's. When you do this, you always come out inadequate. I'll talk more about how to develop your own standards in a bit.

> "Jealousy is comparison. And we have been taught to compare, we have been conditioned to compare, always compare. Somebody else has a better house, somebody else has a more beautiful body, somebody else has more money, somebody else has a more charismatic personality. Compare, go on comparing yourself with everybody else you pass by, and great jealousy will be the outcome; it is the by-product of the conditioning for comparison."
>
> **- Osho**

# Striving For False Superiority

Okay, now that we have looked at why you feel inferior to some people, we are going to examine the other side of the issue.

Maybe when you see someone who is beautiful or popular but unintelligent, you think to yourself: "Yeah, it's true, they've got nothing going for them. I am more intelligent, have a good job, etc..." If your thought process goes something like this, then you are still falling into the comparison trap.

**Now, instead of settling for feeling inferior, you are try to come up with reasons in your mind why other people are inferior to you, and why you are entitled to feel superior. This is still inferiority.**

Let me ask you, when you see someone who is better than you at something, do you feel the need to pull them down from their podium by criticizing? Are you uncomfortable if someone younger than you is more successful than you? Do you feel like you need to put down people you are threatened may be more attractive or more skilled than you?

This process of comparison is usually a very subtle process. You have to pay very close attention to your thoughts and feelings to notice it happening.

**When someone thinks they are inherently inferior in some way, they will overcompensate. Belittle, put down, criticize someone they are jealous of, even if it's only in their own head.** It's a way of reducing the uncomfortable feelings caused by thoughts of inferiority. But all it really does is reveal your own insecurities.

The most obvious example of this is gossip. People only gossip about popular, beautiful, successful, famous people. It's a way of making themselves feel less jealous. Nobody gossips about the homeless person on the street. People only gossip about those they feel their own value threatened by.

> "If you go on condemning, your condemnation shows that somewhere there is a wound, and you are feeling jealous — because without jealousy there can be no condemnation. You condemn people because somehow, somewhere, unconsciously you feel they are enjoying themselves and you have missed."
>
> **- Osho**

The way to overcome feelings of inferiority is not by trying to come up with reasons why you are actually superior. The truth is, trying to make yourself feel superior to others is, like I said before, just revealing an insecurity.

It's similar to when people try to use affirmations to improve themselves. In case you don't know what affirmations are, they're statements like "I'm a valuable and important person" or "I am confident and strong". And the problem with saying these types of statements is that they secretly reinforce the opposite of what you want.

**Think about it. Why would you have to tell yourself constantly that you are valuable and important, unless you secretly believed you were really worthless**

**and unimportant?** Numerous psychology studies support this -- that by trying to suppress or "override" certain thoughts, you just make them come up even more.

> "The irony of thought suppression, then, is that actively trying to manage our own minds can sometimes do more harm than good. Although it makes perfect intuitive sense to try and suppress unwanted thoughts, unfortunately the very process we use to do this contains the seeds of its own destruction. The more we try and push intrusive thoughts down, the more they pop back up, stronger than ever."
>
> **- Dan Wegner,**
> **Harvard Psychologist**

So trying to suppress inferiority by putting other people down and criticizing them in your mind is not going to make you feel any more confident in the long run.

**It's very common for people with SA to fall into this trap of false superiority by thinking that just because they are quiet, that means they are deep intelligent thinkers.** And just because some other people like to go to parties or socialize, that means they are automatically shallow and attention-seeking. Try not to condemn people for having fun or being silly sometimes – don't fall into the trap of looking for ways that you are superior.

# You Are Unique

So if trying to make yourself superior doesn't work, then what does? First you have to realize that inferiority and superiority are two sides of the same coin, and the solution is to realize that the coin itself is false. The truth about you is this:

> You are not "inferior."
>
> You are not "superior."
>
> **You are simply "You."**

"You" as a person are not in a competition against anyone else, simply because there isn't a single other person in the universe the same as you. **Your value comes from your uniqueness as an individual.** Stop measuring yourself against "their" standards. You are not "them" and can never measure up. Neither can "they" measure up to your standards -- nor should they.

You are unique. Once you accept and believe this simple, rather self-evident truth, your feelings of inferiority will disappear.

# On "Real" Inferiority

Sometimes I get people who tell me "But it's not just in my head, I really am inferior to other people." --

Really?

Just because you can't do something as well as someone else does not make you an inferior person. Let me put it this way -- I know for a fact that I am an inferior boxer to Mohammed Ali, I am an inferior actor to Clint Eastwood, I am inferior in some specific area to almost every person I meet, including you.

I know I am inferior to almost everyone in some way or another for a fact, but this does not induce feelings of inferiority within me and make me feel depressed -- simply because I try not compare myself unfavorably with them, and I don't feel that I am no good just because I can't do certain things as skillfully or as well as they can. Similarly, I am probably superior in several ways to all of the people I meet on a daily basis, but that doesn't and it shouldn't make them feel inferior to me.

**Just because you are inferior in doing something, does not make you an inferior person.** It comes down to a core belief that you are not ratable. Your actions can be good or bad, but not you. You can condemn and think low of acts, but not any human beings for any reason whatsoever.

For example, say you make a presentation in front of a group and do poorly. In this case, your performance was bad, but does that mean you are a bad or inferior person?

No, it doesn't. It is essential to rate your performance in order to correct it, but do not rate yourself based on your performance.

> "Imagine you are passing through a garden and you come across a very big tree. If you start comparing, then the tree is so big, and suddenly you are so small. If you don't compare, you enjoy the tree, there is no problem at all. The tree is big -- so what! So let it be big, you are not a tree. There are also other bushes around which are not as big as the tree, but they are not suffering from an inferiority complex. I have never come across a plant or animal which suffers from an inferiority complex or from a superiority complex. Even the highest tree does not have a superiority complex, because comparison does not exist in nature, everything is unique."
>
> **- Osho**

# Fixing Yourself: A Band-Aid Solution

The reason why I'm teaching you to avoid the comparison trap Is so you don't go down the same path most people do. So how do most people try to cure feelings of inferiority? Well, one way is to start trying to fix yourself to make yourself more acceptable to people.

If you have crooked teeth, you may get them fixed. If you are overweight, you go on a diet. If you are ugly, you get plastic surgery. If you are skinny, you start working out. **Whatever you think is a barrier to other people's approval, you try to get rid of.** You start constantly trying to live up to others people's standards so they will (hopefully) accept you.

Although this strategy is better than wallowing in self pity, it is still not a great solution to the problem. You haven't really fixed your self esteem because you're still <u>completely dependent on getting other people's approval</u> in order to feel good about yourself. If other people still have total control over how you feel about yourself, then you haven't really fixed anything.

**The problem with "getting rid of" a perceived inadequacy is that you are not fixing the real flaw -- which is in the way you think!** If you feel like a loser because you are overweight, and you become skinny, then there is always the threat of you sinking back down to being a worthless loser as soon as you gain a few pounds! As soon as you stop meeting the standards, you immediately turn into a worthless loser in your own mind yet again.

Many shy and socially anxious people make the mistake of thinking that if they had just been born looking like a model, then they wouldn't be shy and insecure. This is a huge misconception. People who are confident aren't confident because they have no flaws. They are confident in spite of their flaws.

In fact, their flaws often just make them more unique and interesting. Think about the most confident people you have witnessed in real life and think about the major flaws many of them had. They may have flaws that you yourself would be ashamed of, but they didn't see them as an issue. They didn't feel they needed to be perfect to feel okay. They do not need to live up to other people's standards in order to be able to like and accept themselves.

# Perfectionism

Another common pitfall many people with SA fall into is to rate themselves based on how well they perform in something. You tie up your self esteem in how well you do in school, how well you play a certain sport, how popular you are, how financially successful you are, and so on. If you feel inadequate for these types of reasons, then you are trying to make your behavior, instead of your appearance, live up to other people's standards.

**The "quick fix" for this is to try to perform perfectly.** Try to appear flawless to everyone. Get perfect grades, buy an expensive car, and so on    Avoiding failure, dodging criticism, or attempting to have all your humanly characteristics as being better than average -- all of these are also band aid solutions to the larger problem.

It's not that these solutions don't work    it's just that they usually don't work for long.

## The Leak That Never Plugs

This is the truth which I am trying to help you see. As soon as you fix one "issue" then you'll usually just find a new one to obsess over.

**When someone feels inferiority or shame, they will always find something in their life to justify these feelings. The toxic shame at the root of your bad feelings will FIND something new to hook itself onto.** Whether or not you are good looking, intelligent, fit, successful     it doesn't matter. No matter how good you are, your brain will still distort your perception of yourself negatively.

The real, long-term solution is to fix the way you see yourself, so that you can build a concrete foundation of self esteem that doesn't go up and down like a rollercoaster. Self esteem that doesn't depend on your temporary life situation or whether other people like you at the moment or not.

How can you do this?

I'm about to teach you one of the big secrets for eliminating SA completely, so pay close attention

# The New Way: Unconditional Self Acceptance

I want to teach you a new way to look at self esteem. Really, a much better word for self esteem is UNCONDITIONAL SELF ACCEPTANCE. When you accept yourself, you feel okay just as you are. You feel comfortable with yourself.

**When you are comfortable with yourself, you assume other people will like and accept you. This is the attitude that leads to confident behavior and makes you relaxed around people.**

Next time you are in a social situation, look at the difference between how cool and popular people act and unpopular people do. What is the main difference between them? The popular people accept themselves, and think highly enough of themselves to talk freely and say what they want to say. They are not relying on other people to accept them, because they are already comfortable with themselves. This leads to a stable, relaxed, easygoing attitude in social situations. It leads to a type of social freedom.

The people who are not confident are on edge because, at any second, their acceptance of themselves can drop based on other people's acceptance of them. They are relying on other people to feel good about themselves. Here's some specific examples of how this happens:

- **Insecurities:** Insecurities are a sign of relying on other people for your own inner good feelings. If you are concerned about your looks or any "defect" you have, and constantly check how it looks in mirrors, then you are worrying that the defect makes you unworthy of their approval. (For example, being overweight, having crooked teeth, being too tall/short, etc.) I would also add non-physical insecurities in here as well, like thinking you are too boring or uninteresting.

- **Self-Consciousness:** If you can walk and move normally when alone in your house, but then feel tense and self-conscious in social situations, it's because you are super aware of how other people are seeing you. Instead of letting your legs and body move themselves like you usually do, <u>you are trying to monitor what other people see and think of your actions in real-time</u> and you try to adjust them manually. (By the way, many psychologists think self-consciousness is a misleading name, they prefer to call it "other-consciousness" – which means being overly conscious about how you look from other people's perspectives.)

Do you see how this is really a way that you try to get other people to accept you?

- **Conversations:** If you can speak perfectly fine to close family members, but struggle to think of "the right thing to say" around other people, it's because you are trying hard to get them to accept you. You don't feel comfortable talking freely like you do around the close family member because you are worried that, if you say the wrong thing, they will stop accepting you. So instead of risking disapproval, you weigh every word carefully for its effect to try to control how people will respond to you. This is also the reason why you often say nothing at all in some social situations. (I'll go into this further in a couple chapters...)

**If you think the past few examples apply to you, it means you have conditional self acceptance.** Conditional self acceptance causes self consciousness, inhibition, anxiety, and makes people like you less. When your acceptance of yourself is conditional – this means that you only feel good about yourself when other people like you – then it's like you are a psychological beggar. You are completely dependent on other people for your self esteem and happiness. Other people can usually sense this and it makes you look weak and unattractive.

In case you haven't realized it by now, **shyness and social anxiety are behavioral strategies you've picked up to try to control people's responses to you.** You're trying to make other people accept you. In fact, you are dependent on them accepting you. And the reason why you're so invested in gaining their acceptance and avoiding their disapproval is because you never learned to become comfortable with yourself. You're invested in other people's opinions of you because you are not invested in your own opinion of yourself.

# Living Up To Other People's Standards

If I was going to summarize the basic insecurity problems of people with SA, it would be this: Most people with SA are constantly trying to live up to other people's standards.

They are almost always worried about if their appearance will appeal to others and **whenever they do or say anything, they look to see how other people reacted to decide if it was good or not.** If other people react well, they feel pride. If other people appear to disapprove, they feel shame.

By the way, I am not talking in abstractions here. This "looking for the reaction" is an actual physical behavior in the real world. You can witness it yourself. Next time you see someone shy in a group conversation, look carefully at what they do after they say something. 9 times out of 10, their eyes will dart quickly to the person or people who they feel are the highest social value. It's because they are looking for their approval. Meanwhile, the people who are self-confident will not look for reactions after they talk. Seriously, once you see this happening in the real world, you won't believe your eyes. (As a side note, try to eliminate this behavior in yourself.)

Another example

**Do you ever feel anxious when wearing a new piece of clothing?** Maybe it's nicer than the clothes you are used to wearing and you are worried about people noticing. Or maybe you're dressed very badly, and you are constantly checking and comparing what you are wearing compared to what other people are wearing. This instinct of fitting in is a symptom of a paranoia about living up to other people's standards.

Many people who have social anxiety can't even go eat at a restaurant by themselves or go see a movie at the theater alone. Why? Again, they are paranoid. They don't want someone to have an impression of them as a loner. They are motivated by the need to live up to other people's standards and have people accept them.

By accepting yourself unconditionally, you can finally relax around people fully. You stop being paranoid about your appearance or the clothes you're wearing not being good. You stop being paranoid about avoiding being seen as a loner or making other false "impressions" on people. You stop hiding yourself from other people through strategies I'll talk about in a later chapter.

The opposite of trying to live up to other people's standards is **determining your own standards** about what is the right way to live. If you determined your own standards and decided you were okay by them, then you wouldn't be so anxious to please others with how you act, what you say or how you dress. You wouldn't be so nervous about avoiding disapproval by being quiet, not saying much or not standing out.

People who feel they are low value are usually the ones who feel the need to fit in the most and are constantly managing the impression they make on others. Cut out comparison, and realize that the person who feels high status determines for themselves what is appropriate in the situation. The person with the most self acceptance and firmness in their own standards of living is the one who is least anxious and least invested in the opinions of others.

# Being Filtered Vs. Filtering Other People

**The best way I've found to describe what happens when you start to overcome SA, start to unconditionally accept yourself, and become comfortable with yourself is through something I call "The Filter Switch."** What I mean is that one day you will meet someone and realize that instead of being anxious about whether they like you or if they notice your "defects" and reject you, now you will be instead evaluating whether they meet your standards or not.

Instead of feeling insecure when you look at people's Facebook pages, you will instead be indifferent. You'll instead be focused on communicating to the people you connect with. You'll focus on those people, and not worry about fitting in with the rest.

**Whether other people are good enough for you will become more important than trying to be good enough for them.** And nothing really will have changed objectively about you or about other people.

What did change was your perception of yourself and your value relative to them. It's healthy and normal to screen and filter people we don't know well to see if we want them to become part of our lives. Does this person meet your standards and is capable of fulfilling any of your emotional needs?

This simple change in mindset and self-perception silently seeps into all of your actions and words, affecting everything, without thought or effort. It's no coincidence that when you stop being so concerned with fitting in, people will generally like you more, because you're more likely to be acting authentically. Saying what you want, doing what you want, and being more satisfied with your position in life.

And that's the best description I can think of experiencing self acceptance and comfort with yourself: Which direction is the filter pointing? Are you trying to pass through other people's filter? Or are they trying to pass through yours?

Of course, you'll never be able to master this 100%, but over time this "filter" will become more obvious. There will be a clear feeling in both you and the other person about who is prioritizing who more.

**Which one of you is screening the other person? Which one of you is trying harder to impress the other person? Which one of you is trying to live up to the other person's standards?**

This is not something that you can change overnight. But over time, as you get more social experience, you'll start to take on this mindset more and more. It will likely be a gradual process, a result of a lot of time invested in yourself.It'll be a feeling. Something that slowly shifts your core mode of interacting with people And perhaps you'll occasionally remind yourself: "Wait, why am I trying to prove anything to this person? I don't know them or if I even like them yet."

# How do you Develop Unconditional Self Acceptance?

Here are 6 practical steps you can take today to develop unconditional self acceptance and start living by your own standards. None of these are overnight cures, but they will slowly, over time, correct your way of thinking and develop unshakeable confidence in yourself.

## 1. Stop Forcing Yourself To Perform

**Many people with SA have an attitude towards socializing similar to performance.** They worry that they need to say things which are cool, funny or interesting all the time. They feel like if there is an awkward, silence, then it's their fault and their job to fill it somehow. Or they try to say what they think the other person wants to hear instead of just expressing their true authentic thoughts and feelings. (Trying to say what you think the other persona wants you to say is also called trying to think of the perfect thing to say.) This is why you may sometimes run out of things to say or have a blank mind – it's because you are trying to be a performer.

Once you make the switch in mindset from socializing as a performance to being accepting and comfortable with yourself, you stop performing. Another way to think of this is    you stop trying. Talking to people becomes much easier and more relaxing. You make the switch by expressing your honest thoughts and feelings in the moment, without trying to hide yourself. I'll share a lot of specific steps about how to do this in the next chapter on becoming comfortable with yourself.

**A last note on performance    SA is often caused by commanding yourself that you MUST do well.** When anxious, look for the must. Remember that you don't have to prove anything to anyone, including yourself. For example, if you want to start a conversation with someone new, it's going to be so much easier if you don't think to yourself that it MUST go well or that they must like you.

# 2. Stop Looking To Others

It's funny how your brain tries to trick you. Makes you believe things which aren't true.

One of these "tricks" is confidence.

**When someone is confident, most people automatically assume they have something to be confident about.** You see someone being confident and think there must be something "behind" it. As if they have something figured out that you don't. And that's why they are confident. But it's simply not true.

The truth is

NOBODY KNOWS WHAT THEY'RE DOING Everyone is clueless and scared.

**Stop looking to others to determine what is "the right way" to live.** Realize that there is no "right" way other than the one everyone defines for themselves. There's no right thing to say, no right way to act, no right way to live.

There is no real centralized authority. It's a scattered group of 7 billion people who are all looking at each other. And everyone is looking to and following the person who is most sure of themselves.

It's how fashion gets made. It's how religions are formed. It's how politicians get elected.

As kids we are conditioned to look to others for approval instead of relying on <u>our own sense of individuality</u>. Don't allow your parents, peers, or society to dictate the rules of how you should be. Let go of trying to be someone you are not just to fit in to someone else's model of what is right.

This is the difference between trying to fit into other people's standards versus dictating your own standards in life, which is what confident people do. This goes back to switching the filter I talked about before. Are they filtering you or are you filtering them?

**We are second hand people as long as we rely on seeing the world through the eyes and value systems of other people, who we place on a pedestal above ourselves. As long as we do not see the world through our own eyes, we give up control of our feelings about ourselves to other people.**

# 3. Let Go Of Guilt Or Shame

**Let go of guilt or shame you feel about any natural behaviors/drives you have.** People have a lot of hang ups about their sexuality, eccentricities, kinks, quirks, passions, drives etc because they feel there is something "wrong" with them for having these inclinations.

If something feels natural to you then accept this in yourself fully. Society, advertising and religion tries to brainwash everyone to fit into one average mold, and it just doesn't work. Many people walk around with an inner split – one part of themselves condemning another part. (This is what the famous psychologist Sigmund Freud called the Id and Superego.)

Any guilt or shame you feel within yourself will be felt by people when you talk to them. It will come across in your general attitude or energy. People will catch upon it as a negative vibration in you. They will be able to sense your discomfort with yourself and something will seem "off" about you to them.

# 4. Don't Rate Yourself

**From now on, do not rate yourself in any way, shape or form.** If you do badly on a test or lose your job, it does not mean you are an inferior person. Your worth as a person does not change depending on how well you do and what other people think of you.

You must develop a core belief that you are not rate-able. Your actions can be good or bad, but not you. You just exist. So if you get a bad mark on a test or lose your job, it may mean your actions weren't the right ones, but it says nothing about you. It's essential to rate your performance in order to correct it, but <u>don't rate yourself based on your performance</u>.

# 5. Don't Rate Others

**What goes for you also goes for other people.** Do not rate them. You can condemn acts, but not any human beings for any reason whatsoever. If somebody steals money from you, then their actions were bad, but it does not mean they are an inherently bad or inferior person. If someone shares a different worldview than you, then try to accept that your differences are usually accidental. For example, a Muslim and Christian will have different opinions based on where they were born, and the community they grew up in. But you shouldn't condemn either of them for being ignorant, stupid or wrong – it's just a matter of environment and conditioning.

<u>When you are critical of other people, you will often assume everyone is as critical and judgmental as you are.</u> This will make you care more about what other people think of you. Try to empathize with how others see the world and why they do what they do.

This will paradoxically make you more accepting of yourself because you will realize how fundamentally similar everyone is, instead of being focused on deficiencies and differences.

# 6. Give Up Pride

**You can't give up shame without giving up pride.** They are two sides of the same coin. You can't stop condemning yourself for doing poorly until you stop making yourself feel somehow superior to others when you do well.

Whenever you are thinking of some logical reason why you should feel confident, let it go. The fact that you are more educated, smarter, or more mature than someone does not make you superior to them. The fact that you may have more money or possessions or "more going for you" does not make you superior to anyone. You need to quit the habit of trying to logically convince yourself why you should feel confident. There are no "reasons" to feel confident, because your acceptance of yourself is now unconditional.

**Think of self esteem as something that you were born with, not something that you have to achieve or earn.** You don't have to prove yourself to feel good about yourself. So stop trying to prove yourself, either to yourself or to other people.

---

For each person building self esteem based on an accomplishment, an ability, physical appearance, and so on    they feel good about themselves for as long as their skills, abilities, and accomplishments remain intact. Yet when their skills, relationships, accomplishments and so on change, they lose themselves in the process. Is this self-worth? No, it's "things' worth," not self-worth.

*Have you ever heard of some stock traders who commit suicide when the stock market crashes? Or maybe you've heard about how common it was in the past in Japan for someone who lost their jobs to commit suicide. These people built their self esteem based on their external accomplishments. It's a very psychologically unhealthy thing to do, even if you don't take it as far as these examples.*

This approach to unconditional self acceptance was created by Albert Ellis, one of the most important psychologists of all time. He argued that the only sane and healthy way to live was to accept yourself unconditionally, without rating yourself. He thought the way most people live – feeling good about themselves only if they meet certain conditions – means their life is an unhappy rollercoaster where they feel dissatisfied and inadequate the majority of the time.

> "[...] Give up all your ideas about self esteem, stick only to those of unconditional acceptance, and choose to accept your self, your existence, your humanity whether or not you perform well, whether or not you are loved by significant others, and whether or not you suffer from school, work, sports, or other handicaps."
>
> -Albert Ellis, Ph.D.

# Questions Answered

There are two main questions I get when I teach unconditional self acceptance. They usually go something like this: "If I don't care at all if other people accept me, then won't I just sit at home all day anyway? Won't I lose all motivation to become more social?" and the second one is, "If I don't care about if other people accept my appearance or behavior, then won't I start being rude and abrasive? Couldn't I start punching people if they made me mad and saying things that could lose me my job?"

In other words, if you stop doing things for the need for approval, because you must prove yourself, then why not sit around all day and be completely repulsive to other people?

## Acceptance Does Not Equal Being Passive

Here's the answer to these questions: **You may not NEED other's acceptance in order to accept yourself, but there are still things which you'd PREFER to have, like friends.** Friends are more enjoyable than having no friends, so it's perfectly normal to be motivated to improve your social life because of the pleasure of connection and company.

In the same way, the reason why you shouldn't be completely repulsive to people is not because you fear their disapproval, but because it is advantageous to you. If you prefer to have a job, then it is <u>advantageous</u> to not make your boss angry. But never forget that this is not something that you have to do, only something you choose to do because you enjoy the benefits.

**Having a desire/wish/preference for approval and acceptance is good and normal.** As long as you don't say you MUST MUST MUST have it. Why? Because a lot of the time you won't get what you want, and even if you do, who's to say you'll still have it tomorrow? This is about reprogramming the way your mind works so you can have a stable and sustainable way of feeling okay about yourself.

So although you don't NEED to do anything, there are certain things you'd LIKE to do, and they're no longer driven by a clinging desperateness for people's approval, but from a pure desire to enjoy yourself and have a better existence.

**Your new outlook on life is: "I don't need anything. I just exist. Now what the hell do I do to enjoy myself?"** This is a much better type of motivation than the kind that depends on temporarily filling your addiction to approval through meeting other people's standards for looks, success, and so on.

So instead of feeling ashamed of yourself if you aren't doing as well as you'd like to in some area, say "Ah, such-and-such is a pain in the ass. I wish it weren't so, now what do I do to either change it or live with it?" This applies to lack of friends, lack of romantic relationships, lack of financial success, any insecurities about your physical appearance you may have, and anything else. You no longer NEED them to be different in order to accept yourself, but you can still be very active about improving them.

You improve them in order to increase your own quality or enjoyment of life, not because improving them may make you more worthy of other people's acceptance and approval.

# Need Vs. Preference

**What is the difference between a need and a preference?** When you have a need for something, then you cause <u>emotional conflict</u> in yourself when you don't have it. But if you only have a preference for something, then you are <u>indifferent</u> about not having it.

For example, someone who has a need to be good looking will torture themselves with insecure thoughts when that need isn't being met. Whether they think they are ugly or they just have a bad hair day, they depend on their external appearance to feel good. On the other hand, someone who only has a preference for being good looking may still improve their style, go to the gym, take care of their grooming, and so on    but they still feel okay as they are in this moment.

There is no inner emotional conflict since they have a preference, not a need. They do not need something external to be different to feel at ease on the inside. In fact, this is one of the core teachings of Buddhism. Realizing that suffering usually takes place only when you are trying to make the external world fit into your inner emotional addictions. The solution is to stop trying to fill your emotional addictions, for example the need for approval.

So turn your needs into preferences. **This allows you to accept yourself, but still be assertive about improving your life.** It also removes the inner emotional conflicts and insecurities so many people with SA have.

If this sounds like contradictory advice on the surface, it isn't. To overcome SA, you need a willingness to be assertive and push your comfort zone, as well as the inner belief changes that allow you to become more comfortable with yourself.

Too many people who have shyness or social anxiety only get half of the picture. They decide they should accept themselves, and suddenly feel relieved that they don't HAVE to try being more social anymore or push their comfort zone. But, because they stop being assertive about improving their life situation, they never achieve the goals they want -- like a close relationship, circle of friends, or the ability to speak with confidence.

It's only when you are comfortable with yourself that you can be comfortable around other people. This is one of the big secrets. The first step is to accept yourself unconditionally, and in the next chapter we'll go deeper and talk about other things you can do.

# Chapter 12
# Becoming Comfortable With Yourself

Near the beginning of this book I talked about how toxic shame – the belief that you are "not good enough" to be liked or accepted as you are – is at the core of most people's SA.

The opposite of toxic shame is being comfortable with yourself. In other words, believing other people could like you just for you.

When you are comfortable with yourself, you become comfortable around other people. You feel free to relax and "be yourself" because you assume they will accept you without you having to do anything to alter their impression of you.

In this chapter I'll break down several ways you can build this inner comfort with yourself. But before we get to that, I need to point out two huge mistakes people with SA make. I call them the Turtle and the Chameleon. Both are unconscious strategies to avoid disapproval.

Let me start by explaining the first one

# The Turtle Strategy:
# Are You Secretive And Withdrawn?

Let me ask you a few questions:

- Do you keep to yourself a lot? (Not just in an introverted "I like being alone sometimes" way, but to the point where you don't allow almost anyone to really get to know you.)
- Do you try to hide that you don't really do much interesting activities?
- Do you become anxious if someone asks you about what you did last night or last weekend or what your future plans are?
- Do you keep most of your real interests and hobbies to yourself instead of sharing them with people?
- Do you think if people knew what you actually did 24 hours a day, they would look down on you?

If you answered yes to any of these questions, then don't worry, because you're not alone.

Back when I had social anxiety, I remember being very secretive about my life and what I did in my spare time.

**I thought if someone found out about me having no friends or no social life, they wouldn't like me anymore.** I thought if a girl I liked found out about my lack of past relationships and experience, her interest would disappear before it even started. Basically I thought if people found out about "the real me," then they would instantly reject me.

This caused me to become secretive and withdrawn around people. If someone asked me "what did you do this weekend?" I would try my best to dodge the question and usually I would make the situation awkward. Even though they only asked to try to be friendly, I didn't want them to know I had spent it alone keeping myself amused.

After a lot of time working on my social anxiety, trying to find ways to cure it, and studying the psychology behind it, I figured out the cause of these secretive behaviors.

**Being secretive and withdrawn comes from toxic shame or inferiority.** It's yet another strategy used by your SA to try to avoid disapproval and gain people's acceptance.

You become secretive and withdrawn to avoid being rejected. You may not have any friends if you are this secretive, but you can also avoid the potential for disapproval and rejection. People can't dislike you if they don't know you. So you hide away. Like a turtle.

> "Most people who fear rejection act as though they have some terrible secret that would mean instant loneliness if it were discovered."
>
> **- Jonathan Berent**

When you feel that you are not good enough in some way, then you're going to try to find ways to cover up or compensate for that feeling of inferiority. Usually this happens through trying to create a certain IMPRESSION on someone. Think about this carefully, because it's important

# Trying to Manage "Impressions"

Instead of expressing your personality freely, shame and inferiority make you carefully monitor how other people see you. You spent a lot of time and mental energy trying to make certain "impressions" on people to make them like you.

**In psychology, this is called "impression management".** Impression management is the reason why you try to be seen as someone you're not in front of certain people. And it's also the reason why you may find it hard to share your life and your life and your interests with people.

Here's how the process works: "People can't like me because I'm ugly / loner / pathetic / boring / uninteresting, but if I can create a good impression in their minds, then maybe they will like that impression that I construct."

**In essence, you're trying to "trick" people into liking you. It's all about you trying to make them see you in a certain light.** You're trying to manipulate their perception of you

- If you feel too ugly, you'll only let certain people see you with lots of makeup on or constantly check your appearance in the mirror. You may always be looking down to check your clothes if you see someone you are attracted to.

- If you feel you are a loner, you'll avoid running into people when you're by yourself — you may see them in the distance walking towards you and avoid them. You may also be afraid to go to a restaurant or movie theater alone to avoid being seen as unpopular.

- If you feel like people don't like you because you're too quiet, then when someone you want to impress comes by, you'll try to be louder and more social.

These are all different ways that people with SA try to manage other people's impression of them. Usually, the more high value you think someone is, the harder you will try in this "impression-making."

So you may find it a lot easier to let go and share your interests and "real personality" around someone you don't think is that cool. You may even be willing to reveal parts of yourself you think are unattractive, like saying you have some nerdy hobby like playing videogames a lot. But then around other people, who are more cool, attractive, and high value, you immediately start to manage the impression they have of you.

# The Problem With Impression Management

Right now you may be thinking: "Okay, I now realize I'm trying to create an impression so that people will like me. But what's wrong with that? Is it bad to want to be liked?"

And no, there's nothing wrong with trying to be liked. In fact, every psychologically healthy person does some "impression management", especially in professional situations. **But people who have SA take it too far. They manage impressions to the point where they sabotage themselves from actually communicating and connecting with people. They have a hard time "letting their guard down" even around people they have known for a while.**

There are many flaws with trying to create impressions on people

1) **First,** when other people find out you were <u>putting on an act</u> the whole time, your friendship or relationship will crumble. That's because it was never a real relationship in the first place. It was just you playing a game to get the other person's acceptance and approval. Trying to present yourself to them a certain way to make them like you. Real relationships are formed when you learn to be vulnerable with people.

2) **Second**

> The most miserable and tortured people in the world are those who are continually straining and striving to convince themselves and others that they are something other than what they basically are.
>
> **- Dr. Maxwell Maltz**

3) **And third,** impression management makes you self-conscious and inhibited around people. You don't feel free to express yourself because then you would lose control of the impression you'd make on others. "Impression management" is the opposite of "being yourself." (I'll talk more about this in the next chapter.)

# So What's The Solution?

Is there an alternative to impression management? Yes, there is.

**The solution is becoming comfortable with yourself.** Accepting and coming to terms with yourself just as you are now, with all your faults, weaknesses, shortcomings, as well as your assets and strengths. Accept that you will always be imperfect, just like everyone else.

Once you become comfortable with yourself, you'll stop being secretive because you'll think "what's the point?" If you truly believe that <u>people can accept and like you just for you</u>, then there's no point in wasting so much time and energy <u>trying</u> to make them to like you and avoiding their disapproval.

I'll explain exactly how to do this in a bit, but first I have to tell you about the second big mistake people with SA make, which is

# The Chameleon Strategy:
# Do You Try To Fit In To Get Accepted?

Here are some questions to consider...

- Do you ever find yourself pretending to like certain hobbies or interests because it's popular? This can be sports, fashion, movies, music, drinking alcohol and so on...

- Do you act completely differently around your closest friend than around people you don't know well? For example, maybe you have a wacky sense of humor that you hide around most people? Or maybe you talk about nerdy subjects you find interesting only around that one friend.

- Would you be embarrassed if someone found out what your actual hobbies and passions were? Maybe it's reading, drawing, video games, or something else.

**If you answered yes to any of these questions, then you are probably trying to fit in to get accepted by others.** If you do this, then don't worry, because...

## Again, You're Not Alone

The truth is, almost every shy or socially anxious person does this.

In fact, I did it myself for many years.

I remember back to my childhood, when I would pretend to be interested in whatever the person I was talking to was interested in.

I was always too scared to state my own opinion about something for fear other people would disagree with me. From little things like the latest movie to larger topics like how the world works. I didn't want to create conflict or argument because then people wouldn't like me. Or so I thought.

Sometimes I felt like I would mentally lose my personality around people I was uncomfortable around or didn't know well. The need to fit in would basically take my personality away in these situations and it would literally paralyze me. I would always wonder why I could only act like "myself" around a couple of people I knew very well.

The truth, which most shy and socially anxious people don't realize, is that a lot of their problems come from a subconscious strategy of fitting in. And fitting in is a losing strategy. I'll repeat that to let it sink in.

# FITTING IN IS A LOSING STRATEGY!

When you try to fit in, you are again trying to control how other people see you because you are scared of them rejecting "the real you." This is another form of impression management.

It's another strategy people with SA use to try to make people like them. Instead of hiding away and being secretive, they try to blend in like a chameleon. Both strategies are a form of impression management, and they are both motivated by the fear of disapproval.

So instead of fitting in, the right way to attract friendships and relationships into your life, and create deeply meaningful connections with people is through (what I call) polarization.

# Social Polarization

Have you ever played with two magnets? Did you notice how the magnets would be incredibly attracted to each other sometimes....

While other times they would repel each other completely?

This is called polarization. Polarization is the ability something has to either attract or repel other things. And it's easy to see how it works with magnets, but what you probably don't realize is that it's also true when it comes to socializing and relationships.

**Similar to how a magnet attracts and repels, your authentic personality will naturally attract people only to the extent you're also willing to repel people.** The best strategy to deeply connect with people is to be willing to be polarizing, like a magnet.

If you try to avoid disapproval by fitting in, you become bland, boring and uninteresting to everyone.

So now the question is HOW? How can you use polarization to your advantage?

Instead of trying to change your personality to gain acceptance from everybody, realize that you only have chemistry with certain people. And part of the process of finding the people you have chemistry with is having the courage to slowly open up. How do you do this exactly?

The overall strategy here is progressive exposure and vulnerability. Vulnerability is about letting yourself be seen and opening yourself up to the potential that someone may not like the real you.

## The Internal and External Comfort Zone

Similar to how you have an "external comfort zone" of which social situations you feel comfortable in, you also have an "inner comfort zone". If you want to overcome your social anxiety to the core, it means you have to not just push yourself into more difficult situations, but also expose yourself in progressively more difficult ways.

Pushing the inner comfort zone means exposing more and more of your "real self" to people. Going deeper in what you feel okay sharing. I'm going to give you some tips, but it's going to take time and hard work to rewire your brain and its inner beliefs.

By exposing yourself and seeing that you don't die (which is what your amygdala is wired to believe) you slowly overcome your discomfort with yourself. Your shame and inferiority breaks down as you share and allow yourself to be vulnerable.

**Vulnerability is not about being weak, it's about showing up and letting yourself be seen.** Vulnerability implies inner strength and security, and people usually find it admirable in others, although they are terrified of being vulnerable themselves.

This is not easy. It's dirty work. Here are some tips to point you in the right direction:

# 1. Share your real hobbies and interests with people

Find ways to insert your true passions and interests into the conversation. You never know, the other person may be interested in it as well, or know someone who is.

Commonalities are often great ways to start a friendship. And the more rare the commonality, the deeper the connection usually is.

# 2. Risk your "real personality" getting rejected

Think about the way your talk to your closest friend. The way you joke with them, talk about subjects YOU find personally interesting, and let your true self come out.

Once you have an idea of how you act around them, try to bring that personality more into how you act with everyone.

When you start to do this, you may actually be SHOCKED (like I was) at how many people actually like you. The real you, not the one you keep bottled inside out of fear.

And once you start learning that there is no rejection, only a lack of chemistry, you will find yourself being more willing to open up.

You will find yourself caring less about what other people think, because as a famous person once said

> Be who you are and say what you feel because those who mind don't matter and those who matter don't mind.
>
> **- Dr. Seuss**

# 3. Share your flaws, imperfections and embarrassing stories.

If you have social anxiety, then you probably have some parts of your life which you think are unacceptable to others and must be hidden. Nothing could be further from the truth.

Unless you are a serial killer or have done something legitimately horrible, then the more you share, the better. As you get to know someone over time, make sure you push the limits of what you are willing to share with people. (Obviously different rules for sharing apply at the workplace compared to an informal social gathering.)

**The most dangerous thing to do about something you feel ashamed of is to hide or bury it.**

I remember a couple years ago this guy sharing a very embarrassing story to myself and a few other people. He told us about the time his mother walked in on him masturbating in his bedroom. Most people would try to keep this type of incident a secret and feel guilty about it. And it's probably what I would have done as well. But listening to this guy tell the story really taught me a lesson.

He was comfortable enough with himself that he had no problem telling us this story. And since he obviously didn't feel any shame about it (you could tell by his attitude), the event just turned out to be a funny story instead of a traumatizing incident.

**I'm not saying you have to go this far with sharing, but it's something to keep in mind – when you are comfortable with yourself, you can tell people pretty much anything about yourself and you assume other people will still accept you despite the "flaw".**

It's your attitude that makes the difference. Some people have an insecurity and try to hide it – they are  sensitive to any comment about it. Other people will openly poke fun at themselves for being fat or short or ugly.

For example, I'm shorter than average and if I'm flirting with a girl I just met who is taller than me, then I may point the height difference out. I've even called myself a midget for fun in the past. Many people think height is attractive, but I've found the lack of insecurity is equally attractive.

If you want to hear examples of this, then go listen to some stand up comedians. Many will share the most intimate, embarrassing stories from their lives with huge audiences. Everything from what they do in the bathroom, to their sex lives and failed relationships, to their biggest character flaws and screw-ups. If they can share this with people and still "get away with it," then what makes you different?

Think about the most popular people you know in real life. Chances are, they have no trouble sharing a lot of personal details about themselves openly. This makes them magnetic, because it makes people feel like they know who they are really quickly.

Sharing embarrassing incidents and close insecurities with people allows you to experience people accepting you for "the real you". These real life experiences of acceptance are key to overcoming the toxic shame so many people with social anxiety suffer from.

## 4. Stop hiding your anxiety symptoms.

If you are afraid of other people noticing you blushing, sweating, shaking, or looking nervous, then the solution isn't to put more pressure on yourself to make a good impression. You're already too far invested in the acceptance of other people – the solution is to be indifferent about appearing nervous. Allow other people to know that you are feeling anxious.

One exercise I did for a while when I was overcoming my own social anxiety was telling people "I feel a little bit nervous". You'll be surprised that people don't reject you for being nervous – they are more likely to reject you for trying to present yourself as a bulletproof confident persona when you're not.

This is one of the weird paradoxes of overcoming shyness. **If you start putting pressure on yourself to appear confident in every situation, then you create performance anxiety in yourself in social situations.** As someone who is known for coaching people on overcoming SA, I found myself getting stuck in this trap. In order to become truly confident, you have to be stop caring about always looking confident and impressive. This is the difference between trying to APPEAR not invested in other people's opinion of you, and actually BEING not invested in what other people think of you.

## 5. Pay Attention To When You Get Offended

Similar to sharing your flaws, pay attention to how you feel when other people point out your flaws. If you feel offended by something someone said about you, it just means that you already felt critical about that aspect in you.

**You can't be offended about something you weren't already feeling insecure about.** For example, a skinny guy would never feel insulted if he was called a "fatty" because he knows he is skinny. Only someone who is already feeling sensitive or self critical about their weight would get offended.

The issue is not that someone made a negative comment, the issue is that you are not comfortable with a part of you and therefore became offended. If you were comfortable with all parts of yourself, you would (almost) never feel offended by what others say about you.

## 6. Find a "safe person" to talk to

**Opening up to even one person can be very therapeutic and can cause some serious changes in your level of self comfort.** This is the real reason why a therapist is beneficial to many people. You can talk to them about anything without judgment. The therapist is the first source of unconditional acceptance for many people, which is often the real reason why therapy works.

Other people get the same benefit as talking to a therapist by finding a "safe person". A "safe person" is someone who you can talk to about almost anything. It can be a close friend or family member. They are someone who you can rely on to listen to you without any criticism or judgment. If you are having trouble overcoming your social anxiety, then it can be very beneficial to find a safe person to talk to. Tell them you have social anxiety and are working on overcoming it.

**If the idea of this makes you uncomfortable, it means you should probably do it.** (Remember back to the beginning of the book, where I talked about fear being a compass?) Exposing this real side of you (your authentic feelings) will be uncomfortable at the beginning, but it's something you will get used to. And later you will be relieved that you did it.

> "It is unlikely that a socially anxious person will take the perceived risk of sharing intimate thoughts or feelings, for fear that the acquaintance would find 'the truth' horrifying or even merely unattractive or unacceptable. Most people who fear rejection act as though they have some terrible secret that would mean instant loneliness if it were discovered."
>
> **- Jonathan Berent**

# 7. Go beyond content – connect on motivations

If you feel like all of your conversations tend to be very superficial, then one reason why is because you focus too much on content and too little on getting to know the other person and letting them get to know you.

For example, say you talk to someone and find out they are an engineer and what school they graduated from. These pieces of information are content, they say very little about the actual person, their character and values. To find out about the actual person, you need to ask questions that expose their deeper motivations and values.

**One simple way to do this is to ask "why?"** Why did they choose to become an engineer? Did their parents pressure them into choosing a stable career? Are they analytical by nature? How was it like going to their particular school? Did they party or spend their weekends studying?

By asking these types of deeper questions – questions that go beyond the content of the person's life and address their deeper preferences, motivations and character, you can truly get to know somebody in a relatively short period of time.

**The flip side of this is letting other people know about your own motivations.** For example, if I tell someone I take improvisation theatre classes, they know very little about me. On the other hand, if I tell someone I take improvisation theatre classes to push my comfort zone because I used to be very shy, they will feel like they actually got to know me better.

# 8. Using "I Statements"

"I statements" are another quick techniques you can use to connect with people. "I statements" are basically sentences that begin with "I". They are meant to get you comfortable talking about yourself.

**Any sentence that starts with "I feel ___" or "I think ___" or something similar can be an I statement, as long as you also explain the reason why.**

An example of a bad I statement: "I feel stressed today."

An example of a good I statement: "I feel stressed today because I have an exam later this week and have this important presentation tomorrow ___ and you know how much I hate giving presentations."

The second "I statement" is much better than the first because it also explains <u>why</u> you feel stressed. Going into the why allows you to share yourself instead of sticking to superficial content. "I statements" are an easy way to ease yourself into exposing your inner self to people more. The more you expose yourself to people, the more comfortable you get doing it, and the more comfortable you'll become with yourself.

# 6. Mirror talking exercise

This is an exercise which I think is most helpful to people who have very bad social anxiety. Here's what you do.

When you wake up, look at yourself more while getting prepared for the day. Brush your teeth and stare at yourself in the mirror without blinking. Or if you're not getting out that day, put a mirror beside your computer. Get comfortable looking at yourself in the mirror without feeling weird.

**When you're ready, go look at your mirror again.** Now talk to yourself. Tell yourself about your day. You look pretty damn stupid, don't you? Keep doing it. Spend at least 5 minutes doing it. Talk about your day. A book you read. Some TV show you watched. Whatever.

Do this every day for at least a week and see if it helps you. If it does, keep doing it.

While you're talking to yourself in the mirror, make sure to pay attention to your behavior. Notice how you feel inside, and notice how that comes across in your eyes, facial expression, vocal tonality. Are you uncomfortable even just being with yourself? It's probably a sign that you're feeling negative judgments about yourself. Reread the chapter on unconditional self acceptance and then try this exercise again.

Again, I think this exercise is most useful for people who have really bad social anxiety. It will give you a small first step to get started.

If you want to learn more about shame and vulnerability, a great person to study is Brene Brown. Search Google for "Brene Brown Vulnerability Ted Talk" or check out her bestselling book called "Daring Greatly."

# Chapter 13
# From Self Consciousness To Spontaneity

Many people with shyness or social anxiety are constantly stuck inside their heads.

They are fantasizing or being anxious about what might happen in the future.

They are analyzing something that happened in the past, thinking of what they "could have" or "should have" said.

They are worrying about how other people are perceiving them.

They are thinking, thinking, thinking     their brain is like a hamster that never stops running.

This constant thought and inner analysis is one of your biggest obstacles in overcoming SA. Let me show you the way out.

## Why You Don't Know What To Do

Imagine you're back in high school for a minute. The teacher you hate most has just asked you a question. (Typical of her to pick the only question you don't know the answer to.)

**Suddenly, your mind goes blank.**

What do you do? You desperately try to think of something to say, and an awkward silence falls across the class. They're all looking at you. Everybody's watching.

Suddenly you're not sure where you should put your hands. You move them awkwardly to the back edge of your desk, and you feel how cold and sweaty they are. You have to say something, anything. Quick!

You blurt out an answer. Why does your voice sound so weird? Everyone keeps looking at you for some reason.

You wish the teacher would move on with the other people in the class...

# What Did You Do Wrong?

Maybe that situation has happened to you before. Maybe it's happened to you many times. Or maybe some other, similar situation has happened. It's happened to me, and it happens to most people who have SA, for a reason.

The reason is you tend overthink and be preoccupied about what other people think of you. In the classroom, you were very aware that everyone was watching you. You didn't want to mess up.

You didn't want other people to get the wrong impression of you, so you had to think carefully about what you were going to say or do next. You tried to plan your words and actions carefully. Unfortunately, your plan backfired horribly.

# You Fell Into A Trap

It's a trap many people with SA get caught up in. They try to micro-manage and control what other people think of them. **They continually think about little things that are unimportant.**

For example, here's the process shy and socially anxious people go through before they say something:

- First they ask themselves "What should I say next?"
- "Will it sound good?"

- "What's the best way to say it?"

  They may even pre-rehearse what they're going to say.

- And only then do they (sometimes) actually say it.

**This type of behavior is called <u>Self-Monitoring</u>, and it's bad for several reasons:**

First of all

# 1. You Hesitate

Instead of just letting go and expressing yourself, you think and think and think. And when you finally do something, it feels unnatural. It's not fun for you and it's not fun for other people.

Here's something to keep in mind:

**The more you hesitate before doing something, the more contrived and phony it will seem when you finally do.**

For example, if you think of something to say, and then wonder if you should say it, you get nervous. The more you wait, the more nervous you get. It stops becoming something that just popped into your head and starts becoming YOUR own idea. You put more and more importance on how people will react to it. When you finally do say it (IF you actually say it) it usually sounds unnatural. You spent too much time and attention controlling how you act, and it comes out wrong.

The second reason why self-monitoring is bad, is because

# 2. You Seem Out Of Focus

When you Self-Monitor, you seem out of focus. Like you're actually 10 seconds in the past or 10 seconds in the future.

Only shy people and those who are extremely self-conscious closely monitor what they say and do. The average person doesn't monitor what they do, at least not in casual conversations. What most people do, is not think at all before they act or speak.

This doesn't mean they have no idea or control of what they will say or do next. But they don't think about the <u>exact words</u> of what they're going to say next. **They get a general feeling of what they want to communicate, and they say it.**

This is a more direct and open way of communicating. It's the difference between a job interview where both people feel a little formal and awkward and a conversation with a close friend which feels completely natural and comfortable.

Often when I tell this to people with SA, they feel confused. If they don't know exactly what they are going to do before they do it, then couldn't they start spewing nonsense and repelling everyone? And is it really a good idea to become one of those loud, obnoxious people who say everything without thinking first?

Once you learn how to stop self-monitoring, I guarantee you'll change your mind. You'll find that letting go of needing to tightly control everything you say will actually make you communicate better. It will be like you've been driving your whole life with brakes on socially, and just now you discovered how to release your brakes.

Think back to one of your best experiences socially. Chances are, it felt like the right words were somehow coming out of your mouth automatically. You weren't stuck in your head, trying to come up with something to say. It was all flowing, and you felt in the moment and connected to the other person. Best of all, it was effortless, so you were having fun. Learning to become more spontaneous takes the effort and work out of being social.

And the third reason why self-monitoring is bad is

# 3. You Seem Inauthentic

Oh, the irony. You want people to like you and think you're a good person, but they don't. They think you're inauthentic.

**When you monitor everything you say and do, it doesn't come from you directly.** It's been filtered by your mind, and people can feel it. They can sense the slight off-ness when you've been thinking of a remark for a minute. **They don't feel the same energy coming from you as from a person who comes up with something to say on the spot, and that lack of energy turns them off.**

If you find that other people don't really seem to like talking to you, then it could be that they are being repelled by your self-monitoring. Unconsciously, they know that someone who isn't being spontaneous see themselves as low value and your inauthentic behavior is being driven by a need to avoid their disapproval.

Basically, any time you are trying to create some sort of impression on people, you are sabotaging yourself, because they can usually pick up on it subconsciously. And only someone needy and desperate for approval would be trying so hard to make other people perceive him well. On the other hand, if you don't really care about the particular impression you make on someone, and you are able to be more free and spontaneous, it shows that you are secure in yourself because you don't require other people to approve of you. You feel okay saying what's on your mind instead of trying to figure out what other people would find interesting or amusing to hear.

Don't worry, I'll talk about specific techniques you can use in just a bit.

# Self-Monitoring Causes Self Consciousness and Inhibition

Let's think about what self-monitoring actually is. Self-monitoring is when you're trying to consciously control actions and behaviors that are normally unconscious. What does that mean?

I'll use your breathing as an example. Most of the time your breathing is an unconscious behavior. You are not conscious of it because your body takes care of it without you having to do anything. But if you started to make yourself breathe differently, quicker or deeper, you have now made breathing into a conscious behavior.

Now you are paying attention to it. It's like the difference between letting an airplane run on autopilot versus taking control of it using the steering wheel.

**So the point is, you self-monitor when try to take control of behaviors that should happen on their own.** You control them because your SA makes you want to control the impression you're making to avoid disapproval.

Here's some examples

- Do you control how you move your mouth when you talk?
- Do you think about how your arms and legs move as you walk or sit down?
- Do you worry about what position your arms are in?
- Do you plan out the exact words you're going to say before you start talking?

Maybe you aren't doing it now, but in tough social situations you do it.

I often get people who ask me things like "How can I walk/speak more naturally?" The problem is, they are usually looking for some tip they can use to <u>force</u> their walk to be more natural. Or to <u>force</u> their voice to sound more pleasing to other's ears. **What they don't realize is that the fact they are even thinking about this is what's causing the problem to begin with!** Most actions that relate to socializing should come naturally and instinctively, not by conscious effort.

**You should control the <u>intent or purpose</u> behind your words and actions, but not all the little details of what exact words or movements you will do.**

Your eventual goal should be to socialize naturally. What gets in your way is self-monitoring and overly controlling your actions. This is what causes you to become self-conscious and inhibited. So don't consciously force your mouth to move when you're talking. Don't try to make your arms to move a certain way when you're walking. Don't try to script and pre-rehearse the exact words you're going to say. Let go control and allow them to do what they may.

I hope this doesn't sound too hard or complicated to do. It really isn't. It's more about learning to become comfortable and relaxed in general social situations. Learning to focus on the right things and realize when you're paying attention to the wrong things.

Part of this "let go" will come just by simply learning to be more physically and mentally relaxed in social situations. That's the foundation. How do you become relaxed? Exposure and the relaxation techniques I taught you in parts one and two, combined with time. Becoming comfortable and accepting of yourself will also allow you to let go and relax more.

But there's also some more direct methods to stop self monitoring as it comes up. These methods are useful for immediately breaking the old bad habits of over-thinking, over-analyzing and over-monitoring yourself in social situations.

# 6 Tried-and-True Methods To Stop Self-Monitoring

First you have to realize when you are self-monitoring. You have to "catch yourself in the act." This can be hard at first. When you realize you are self-monitoring, you then have to...

## 1. Switch your focus.

**Your attention never stops. It can't be shut off or lowered, only directed.** One of the most important things you can do to overcome your SA is to focus your attention in a way that will serve you instead of holding you back.

In a social situation, if you worry about all the things you might be doing wrong, and are focused on not embarrassing yourself, you will end up "playing it safe." You might say as little as possible and when you do speak, you'll be self- conscious and it'll come across weird. But if your focus is on getting to know others and sharing a good time with them, you will fit right in and people will accept you into the group.

**If you are totally immersed in a conversation so that all you are thinking about is what is being discussed, then the words will come automatically and spontaneously to you.** Total immersion in the conversation is something most people with good social skills do naturally from childhood, but people with social anxiety need to learn and practice it. Again, this is a simple shift of focus.

If you are just walking by yourself and feeling self-conscious, you can still switch your focus to something else. Think about a project you're working on. Observe and become fascinated in the environment around you. Think of something that will take your mind completely off what you're doing physically.

It's only possible to be self-conscious when you are preoccupied with yourself. Preoccupation means focusing on you. So switch your focus onto something external. Remember that only people who believe themselves to be low value are constantly "keeping track" of how others are seeing them.

I'll talk more about focus in the next chapter. The second thing you can do to stop self-monitoring is

## 2. Stop talking to yourself.

If you're constantly talking to yourself in your head, stop. Outgoing people talk to other people. **Shy and socially anxious people talk to themselves, especially when they are avoiding talking to other people.**

It's okay to talk to yourself when you are alone, or thinking about some issue you want to solve. But if you continue the habit of talking to yourself even in situations when you want to be more social, then you are just sabotaging yourself.

**Talking to yourself too much takes you out of the present moment and situation you are in.** It disconnects you from other people and can make you "stuck in your head," which means <u>you think so much you put yourself into a not talkative state</u>. The more you talk to yourself, the more comfortable you become being silent, and you turn into the quiet person who rarely says anything. Talking to yourself becomes a sort of comfort zone and a form of partial avoidance.

So how to fix it? First you have to realize when you are talking to yourself. Most people who have SA are not even aware of the voice in their head. Start to pay attention to that voice. (Hint: It's probably going on non-stop, even as you're reading this.) When you are in social situations, switch your focus like I showed you in method number one.

When you quiet your mind and put your focus on the situation in front of you, you will find yourself becoming much more likely to say something. Why? Because you get bored. It's that simple. If you don't talk to yourself, then just sitting or standing there will become boring. When I started quieting the voice in my head I would start to speak up more just to stop being bored. It was my only option.

When you are not talking to yourself, your attention becomes focused in the real world, instead of daydream-land. You start to feel a lot more connected to other people, and they will respond to you better. You start to feel much more engaged and immersed in conversations, which means you'll be able to keep conversations going much easier.

The reason why this happens is because you've given yourself no choice but to have your attention focused in the present moment. Not talking to yourself takes you out of fantasy and into reality. When you are "in the present" or "in the now", then magical things happen to your social skills. I'll talk more about this in a later chapter.

The third tip to stop self-monitoring is

# 3. Don't Pre-Rehearse What To Say

In most situations, you should not wonder in advance of what you are going to say. **The worst thing to do is rehearsing what you are going to say in your head before you say it.** Trying to plan the perfect thing to say or think of the best topics to talk about before you enter a conversation is a crutch you should get rid of.

Most people just get a general gut-feeling of wanting to say something, and they open their mouths and say it. They go with expressing the feeling in their body, rather than trying to rationally plan every move. Don't plan - act first, then correct your actions as you go along if someone misunderstands you.

**Keep in mind that casual conversations are a free exchange of thought and feeling.** They are never perfect, like a movie script. If you wrote down the average conversation people have, you would see how messy it usually is. Full of ums and ahs, people correcting what they meant to say, and jumping on different conversational topics. If you tried to plan it all out, then you would go crazy.

The fourth tip to overcome self-monitoring is

# 4. Don't hesitate

**When a thought pops into your head, express it within 2 seconds.** The longer you wait the worse your fear of expressing it badly becomes. You build it up too much in your mind. The solution is to downplay. You could be in a war zone right now. Instead, you're just talking to people.

**Being spontaneous is a muscle, the more you use it the easier it becomes to rely on it.** At first you will probably feel a "block" to just saying something you thought of. But as you try this technique out a few times, you will find it easier and easier to say things spontaneously. You'll learn to start trusting yourself. You will realize through experience that when you express what you really want to say in the moment, people will usually react well.

# 5. If you don't say something, then let it go.

In the beginning it will be tough to break the habit of hesitation. So go easy on yourself. Many people with SA will wind up obsessing over not saying something they could have for hours or days afterwards.

My best advice is if you hesitate too long to say something, then just let it go. Stop thinking about it and bring your focus back to whatever is now being talked about. Once you've hesitated for too long, then chances are you'll probably never say it. That moment will never come back. Let it go. Next time something pops into your head, try to say it within two seconds.

The last tip for stopping self-monitoring is

# 6. Don't criticize your actions.

**After you do something, do not analyze how well it went.**

Here's how a typical inhibited person acts: after they have finally gotten up enough courage to say something, they immediately start criticizing themselves afterwards. They may say to themselves, "Maybe I shouldn't have said that. Maybe I sounded strange. Maybe the other person will take it the wrong way."

Stop being so self-critical.

**Your criticism is unnecessary because when you make a mistake in a social situations, your mind learns the lesson and automatically adjusts your future behavior.**

It's the same as learning to ride a bicycle. If you fall, your brain gets feedback from the experience. Over time, you learn how to keep your balance and not make the same mistakes again. Learning social skills works the same way as learning balance. You may start out awkward    you say jokes at the wrong time    people look at you like you're weird sometimes. It may feel bad, but it's the way you make progress. Over time, your brain continually learns from your experiences and improves your behavior automatically based on the feedback you get from interacting with other people.

So stop criticizing every little thing you say and do and beating yourself up. **Useful and beneficial feedback works subconsciously, spontaneously, and automatically.** Constantly criticizing yourself on a daily basis is not helpful. There is no benefit. It just makes you feel bad and lowers your self esteem for the future. Allow yourself to make mistakes when learning social skills.

There you go. Six proven methods to cut down on self-monitoring. I guarantee that, by putting them into action, you'll see great results. Here's answers to a couple common questions I hear about this new method of being spontaneous. The first one is...

# "But What If I Say Something Embarrassing?"

This objection does make sense on the surface. If you don't run through whatever you're going to say in your head, how do you know what you're actually going to say?

My answer is

**When you're talking spontaneously, you still will have control over <u>what</u> you are trying to communicate, it's just that you aren't trying to tightly control <u>how</u> you express it.**

Beyond that, you just have to trust that over many years of conversation and hearing other people talk, you have enough knowledge to be able to act appropriately in most situations without consciously filtering everything you say. This takes a leap of faith at the beginning.

You've been thinking about what to say for so long, that just talking without a filter will seem unnatural at first. Trust me, it's much easier and it's how most people actually talk.

The other common question is...

# "Isn't Some Inhibition Good?"

One common piece of feedback I receive when I teach this to people is they'll say to me: "But isn't being totally spontaneous and uninhibited bad? I mean, if I completely didn't care what people thought, then I might go around insulting and offending everyone and then nobody would like me."

How do I respond to this?

**Yes, the world does need a certain amount of inhibition. But not you.** The key words are "a certain amount." <u>You</u> have such an excessive amount of inhibition, you are like someone with a fever telling me that some temperature is necessary for people to stay alive. If you have a fever, the best thing to do is to focus completely on reducing your temperature. Don't worry about your temperature being too low, that's not your issue right now.

In fact, there are some people who could benefit from being more inhibited. Some people in the world really should "think before they speak" more. But if you are reading this book, that's not you. You need to focus on disinhibiting yourself. The "cure" to inhibition and self-monitoring is in taking a long step in the opposite direction.

**By focusing solely on disinhibiting yourself and reducing overthinking, you are working against your current habit of hesitation, and what winds up happening is that you wind up somewhere in the middle.**

It's really impossible to totally not care what other people think of you. You will always care no matter what, it's built into every psychologically healthy person. Your brain will always be monitoring what you say at some level.

For example, do you notice how some people will use swear words around friends, but never at work? This is a way people are able to control their behavior to be appropriate to the situation without having to monitor every single word they say. It happens automatically. So do not worry at all about being "too uninhibited", only focus on practicing being less careful, less concerned, and less conscientious of your actions.

It's like a basketball player practicing jumping. His coach tells him to "jump and touch the sky." Of course, he will never reach it, but by focusing on trying to do it, he will jump a lot higher than if his goal was just to get 3 feet off the ground.

# From Impression-Making to Authenticity

There's one last idea I want to touch on. I've been hinting at it throughout this entire section. The idea is that spontaneity allows you to express yourself much more authentically.

Like we said above, self-monitoring comes from shame or inferiority. You don't think that people would accept you for who you truly are so you feel the need to alter people's impression of you.

**Becoming authentic means removing the gap between the persona you try to put out to the world and your real "core" personality.** It means letting go of needing to make any sort of impression on the people you interact with and just expressing your real personality freely.

# Connecting To Your "Natural" Personality

What I am trying to get you to do here is to get in touch with the way you naturally act when you don't feel the pressure of other people's eyes on you.

Do you ever notice how at home you walk completely relaxed and normal, yet become self conscious in public?

Or maybe you have one or two people who you can "be yourself" around, but when you try to talk to other people you don't know what to say?

Many people who I teach often assume that they need to learn some new social skills to improve their personality. This isn't true at all in most cases. **Most of the time, it's not a question of adding anything to your personality, but removing the barriers which hold you back.** Your fears, self-consciousness, and inhibition. Once these are removed in a given situation, you'll find that expressing yourself is both simple and enjoyable, and it requires almost no thought.

Ironically, the best way to make people like you is not to try to make them like you. The best way to make people like you is to express your personality freely without worrying about possible disapproval. The way to make a good impression is to never consciously try to make a good impression. Let whatever happens, happen. Leave it up to fate, but do not try to control other people's reactions to you by changing your behavior. Never "wonder" consciously what the other person is thinking of you, or how they are judging you.

# Saying "The Right Thing" Vs. Believing In What You Say

What stops you from just saying whatever comes to mind? Well, there are several reasons. Some are good, and others are bad.

There's some good reasons for not saying something. For example, maybe you want to be considerate, not offend others, or not lose your job. But most of the time your reasons are based in fear and self-doubt. **Often times it is an issue of how <u>entitled</u> you feel to speak your mind around the people you are with.**

When you have shyness or social anxiety, you will either not say anything at all or you will carefully weigh every little thing you do for its effect. You are trying to "say the right thing." You may only speak up when you think of something very funny or entertaining or insightful to say.

Although it's not a bad thing to be funny or entertaining when you talk, it's also important to feel comfortable talking to people and having a "normal" everyday conversation. This is something shy people tend to have trouble with.

Instead of trying to say the perfect thing all the time, start to lower the bar on what you allow yourself to say. Express your thoughts and opinions and share how you feel about things.

Once you start to value yourself more as a person and build your own self esteem, this will become much easier. You'll start to truly believe that people can like you just for you, instead of always needing to make some funny comment to keep their love and attention.

Here's the truth    What you say doesn't have to be that funny or interesting most of the time. In fact, it usually just exposes the fact that you think you have to entertain people for them to want to be around you.

If you are ever wondering "What's the right thing to say in this situation?", STOP. **Start to install the belief that what you say is the right thing to say, not because it's a great comment, but because it comes from you.** Don't be afraid to say things that are boring or obvious. People are perfectly satisfied talking to another, regular, normal person.

## People Don't Remember Most Conversations They Have Anyway

Listen to the types of conversations most people have. Sure, some of them are about interesting topics or very funny, but the point of most conversations is just for people to enjoy each other's company.

I have some friends who I have very interesting conversations with,. But not every conversation is super-deep or witty. It's just not a reasonable expectation. Most people talk because connecting and relating with other people is a basic human need. At the end of most conversations most people can barely remember what they even talked about. They may only remember one or two points a week later, or they may never revisit the conversation again mentally.

**The content of the conversation wasn't that important**, the main thing was just to share each other's company. It's an energetic exchange, not an intellectual give-and-take. Unless you have some friends you really like to discuss deep topics with – that can be extremely rewarding as well. But it's important to set low expectations for what you feel comfortable talking about in day to day conversations, or else you'll rarely speak. You won't be able to form relationships because you won't be around people long enough or often enough for that bond to form.

Learn to get in touch and express the gut feeling in your body, instead of self-monitoring and over-analyzing. Most people who have SA become so analytical that their connection to the feelings inside their body is cut off. If you're ever in doubt about what to do, remember that the key is to get in touch with your inner feeling and act more instinctively.

# Chapter 14
# Mindfulness and Being Present

In this chapter I'm going to share with you a few of the biggest practices that helped me to overcome social anxiety. I'm going to teach you techniques that will allow you to quiet your anxious thoughts, naturally put you into a state of relaxation instead of tension, and allow you keep your attention completely in the present moment, which is a foundation of confidence.

Some of these ideas are central teachings of Buddhism and Zen. Others are adapted from various cutting-edge therapy programs. Combined, they form a powerful set of techniques to help you with overcoming SA. Make sure to listen to this chapter or read it several times to truly understand the ideas fully.

I'm going to start with explaining how Mindfulness works...

## Swimming In Our Thoughts

Most people are like fish swimming in their thoughts. When fish swim, they don't know they are underwater, they just swim. Thinking is the same for most people. Our thoughts are like the water.

**We are so immersed and caught up in our thoughts most of the time that we hardly realize they are there.** Although we are thinking all the time, we almost never consciously notice we are thinking.

Thinking, for most people, is an unconscious and automatic process. We pay no attention it. Do you have to think about blinking or breathing most of the time? No, you just do it.

Because most people think in an unconscious and automatic way, they become incredibly wrapped up in the <u>contents</u> of their thoughts. They allow their mind to drag them around to wherever it wants, never realizing that they actually have very little control over the types of thoughts they have.

A well-known author called Eckhart Tolle has described the way most people think as being compulsive and uncontrollable. I think he's right. Most people believe that they control what their mind thinks about, but when you stop and do mindfulness, you soon realize that most of your thinking happens on autopilot, and it happens in reaction to the environment.

**Mindfulness is about putting careful attention onto your thoughts.** By doing so, you are able to gain an awareness and perspective you didn't have before. It's like the fish realizing for the first time that it is swimming in water. Suddenly, you aren't swimming in your thoughts anymore. You have jumped out of the fishbowl and are able to observe your thoughts swimming around inside the fishbowl.

# "What's The Point?"

If you are wondering what benefits mindfulness will have for your SA, then I'll tell you.

First of all, mindfulness is incredibly helpful for those with anxiety because it creates distance between you and your negative thoughts. **You are able to observe your anxious thoughts from the outside**, instead of being INSIDE your anxious thoughts and looking at the world through the lens of your anxious thoughts.

And it doesn't just help with anxious thoughts, but also thoughts that make you feel depressed, insecure or self conscious. New breakthrough forms of therapy like Mindfulness-Based Cognitive Therapy and Acceptance and Commitment Therapy have been scientifically proven to work, and the main tool they offer is developing this perspective through mindfulness.

Secondly, **mindfulness is the stepping stone to learning how to be present in the moment** instead of constantly thinking about the past, or fantasizing about the future.

If people have ever told you that you zone out or daydream often, then you need to learn how to live more in the present. By practicing mindfulness and becoming more present to the moment, you'll find yourself being seen as much more confident and charismatic. Facing your fears will become much easier. And you will gain an emotional stability and centeredness you never had before.

# Mindfulness In A Nutshell

So how to become mindful? The technique is deceptively simple, but not easy. **All you do is observe your thought process without interfering with it, judging what you observe, or commenting on it.** Just allow your mind to chatter on about whatever it likes, and your only goal is to remain a detached observer or witness of what happens.

I've read one book describe this as imagining that your stream of thinking is like a train and you are just watching the train cars pass by.

**The process of mindfulness is simple to write down, but not easy to practice.** I've just given you all the basic steps. So the important thing to know is that you have to practice it. It's an experiential exercise that you need to actually do to see results. Just reading ABOUT mindfulness without doing it will accomplish nothing. It takes time to rewire habitual patterns, especially compulsive thinking. But as long as you get the basic concept of it, then it's only a matter of time and practice. It's a matter of sitting down and observing your thinking.

What you'll find when you try this is that, although you can do it for a few seconds, you quickly lose focus. You'll forget about only observing and start to get involved with your thoughts automatically. This can be very frustrating in the beginning. But you just have to stick with it even though you will suck at mindfulness.

The process of learning to do mindfulness involves making thousands of these mistakes where you lose awareness. When this happens, just go back to witnessing and being aware of your thoughts without involving yourself in them.

Remember that mindfulness is all about detached observation of your thought processes.

If you do it right, you'll find that **you have started to create a gap between you and your thoughts**. You are no longer able to be mindlessly pulled around by your thoughts as you were before. You can now see the water you've been swimming in all your life. It's a shift towards looking at your thoughts, instead of looking at the world through your thoughts.

By practicing mindfulness and creating this gap, you'll get so many benefits when it comes to SA. First of all, you'll stop listening to the automatic negative thoughts (ANTs) that your mind comes up with all time. These are thoughts which come from the mindset of shame, inferiority and anxiety. You'll find that you'll become more relaxed, and you will feel more positive and joyful instead of depressed. Mindfulness has been scientifically proven to prevent depression from happening to people    even those who had a past history of clinical depression!

It's all about creating and deepening that gap between you and your thoughts. Creating the perspective of a detached observer who does not judge, comment or interfere with the thoughts. Simply observe them. Observe them as if you were looking inside someone else's mind. That will be enough to transform you.

If you've ever tried cognitive behavioral therapy, you'll know that most traditional types of therapy tried to change people's thoughts through journaling and challenging irrational thinking. In other words, they tried to change the <u>content</u> of your thoughts. What modern therapies based on mindfulness have found is that it's not really necessary to change the content of your thoughts. It's simpler and very effective to <u>change your relationship to your thoughts</u>. You change your relationship to your thoughts by becoming the outside observer and watching your mind, instead of being pulled into every single thought and viewing them as being generated by you.

# Mindfulness To Become Present

So far I've only described one type of mindfulness. Mindfulness of your thinking. But there are lots of other types of mindfulness where you pay attention to other things, like your body or the environment.

The great thing about these other types of mindfulness is that they allow you to become present to the moment and you can do the exercises in almost any situation. What do I mean by being present?

**Once you start observing your thinking, you'll realize that 99% of the time, you are either reliving the past through memories, or trying to imagine or project how something will be in the future.** You are almost never actually keeping your attention in the real world. You are almost never living in reality, which is the present.

I'll explain this more in a bit, but most of the time when you feel anxiety, it's because you are disconnected from reality. If you are feeling anxious about having to talk to someone in one hour, then you are feeling anxious about a situation that does not exist now. And if you are suffering because of something that does not exist, then it's almost like a form of insanity. I believe that a lot of the worry, stress and anxiety most people experience could be fixed if they would just learn some techniques for mindfulness.

Here's a couple of mindfulness techniques:

- Feeling the sensation of yourself sitting in the chair. Really hold your attention onto HOW it feels. Or the sensation of your feet on the ground.
- Keeping your attention on the sounds of the environment. Noticing all the little details you didn't pick up on before.
- Hold your attention on the sensation of your breathing. Feel how the air goes in and out as you breathe.

**The main challenge with these types of mindfulness exercises is to NOT start thinking about it.** The point is simply to practice developing and expanding the amount of attention you put into the present. You're grounding yourself into reality, the reality of what's actually real and happening right now.

# Living "Moment-to-Moment"

If "being present" is a hard idea to grasp, then think of this as learning how to live moment-to-moment. Living moment-to-moment means to have the majority of your attention focused on the present situation you are in, without thinking. It means being focused on the reality of what is happening right now, instead of the illusion of your thoughts.

Why do I called your thoughts illusions**? Because the future in your mind is not real.** It is just a collection of thoughts. These thoughts can cause anxiety and fear if you imagine something bad happening in the future, or hope if you imagine something good happening. Either way, the future you imagine is not real, because it is only happening in your head.

**Your thoughts about the past are also not real.** When you think about your past, you are reliving something that happened before. It may be true that you are thinking about a real event that happened, but the point is the actual event is not happening right now.

**If you are often reliving something that happened 10 years, 10 months, 10 minutes or even 10 seconds ago, then you are not able to focus on the only place where your actions can make a difference, which is the present.**

You can't affect the past or the future. I remember when I was learning to play a new instrument. A good friend told me: "If you mess up or play the wrong note, forget about it! It's done man, you can't go back to that. The river keeps flowing. Stay in the present!"

This is exactly the mindset you must be in when you are talking to someone or a group of people, especially if you have issues with anxiety or fear. You have to realize that you can't affect the past or future, **you can only deal with the situation that's directly in front of you.** If you mess up, don't think about it! Bring your attention back to what is happening right now, not what happened a couple minutes ago. Plenty of people say dumb things occasionally, but it doesn't matter to them because they don't dwell on it. They forget about it almost immediately and just stay with the conversation.

If you are thinking of something that may happen in the future, like what you're gonna say, then stop that as well. It kills your spontaneity and delivery. Don't pre-plan what you are going to say. You have to start trusting that what you are going to say will come to you naturally when, and only when, you need it. All you need to do is to keep your focus in the present moment as it unfolds.

If you often have trouble with feeling anxious before an event, like talking to someone on the phone or going to a party, then I've just given you the best solution. I've shown you the cure to anticipatory anxiety     and that is by using mindfulness exercises to ground yourself in the present.

# How Presence Reduces Anxiety

**The greatest benefit to learning how to be present for people with social anxiety is being able to become present whenever you are feeling anxious.** All of the techniques I talked about for reducing anxiety -- diaphragmatic breathing, muscle relaxation and acceptance -- are supercharged if you can combine them with being present.

Here's an example. If you are walking to work or school and feeling anxious of what might happen or a conversation you're gonna have, try this exercise. Place your attention onto the bottom of your feet. Feel the sensation there as you walk. How does it feel? Stay WITH the sensation. This is the hardest part. If you slip back to thinking or fantasizing about what's going to happen (which you will), then make sure to go back to awareness. Go back to staying aware of the naked sensation at the bottom of your feet. This technique will ground your attention to the present moment, once you get good at it.

**When you become present, your anxious thoughts simply stop.** Worry and anxiety are both caused by anticipating something bad is going to happen. They are caused by thinking about some situation in the future and projecting a bad outcome. When you are present you don't have these issues because the totality of your focus is now centered on the moment in front of you. In this state, it becomes a lot easier to face your fears. You may still have some anxious feelings running through your body, but they will be a lot easier to handle. They won't sabotage you like they did before.

# Presence Is Not Thought Suppression

One of the comments I sometimes get when I teach this is: "So you're basically saying to suppress my anxious thoughts?" The answer is no. Thought suppression is not something I teach.

**In order to stop thinking and become present, you should NOT try to suppress or fight your thoughts**. In fact, you should do the exact opposite. Allow your thoughts to wander wherever they like. Accept whatever you are feeling, even if it's unpleasant. This goes back to the chapter on acceptance.

All you must do is become the observer behind your thoughts or feelings. Watch your train of thoughts as it passes by, but do not try to stop, control, judge or interpret them in any way whatsoever. Simply observe.

When you aren't familiar with mindfulness, then you won't believe that this can actually do much good. But it's actually a very powerful process, if done correctly and consistently over several weeks or months. You don't actually have to do anything. Just pay attention.

Here's your homework assignment:

**Follow the instructions on mindfulness and being present in this chapter.**

1. Sit down for 20 minutes a day across from a blank wall.
2. Set up a timer so you do not need to constantly check the time.
3. Observe your stream of thoughts. Don't judge, comment on or analyze your thoughts.

4. Once you get the hang of it, try out the other mindfulness exercises I talked about here. Mindfulness of the physical sensations of your body are great, like paying attention to the feeling at the bottom of your feet. Or pay attention to all the little sounds in the environment you didn't notice before.

5. Make this into a 20 minute a day habit and it will change your life. Make you calmer, more relaxed, more mentally and emotionally stable, and happier. Set aside some time right before you wake up to do this. (Or right before you go to sleep.)

6. Review this chapter regularly to make sure you are practicing correctly. Once you get the hang of being mindful by yourself, start to use the technique in your daily life. Become more and more present in every area of your life. Learn to do it when you are hesitant about facing an anxiety-provoking situation.

I hope you understand what I have told you here because it really changed my life. And you "understand" it by doing it. Not just by reading about it. Once you become present, then anxiety will have lost most of its control over you. You may still feel it, but you will be much more free to take the steps needed to get rid of it.

The most important thing is to STICK with it daily. Don't just do it 2 or 3 times and get lazy. To give you some additional motivation, let me share with you a few results from scientific studies.

# Many More Benefits to Mindfulness

Did you know that meditation is scientifically proven to

- **Overcome stress** (University of Massachusetts Medical School, 2003)
- **Boost your creativity** (ScienceDaily, 2010)
- **Improve your sex life** and increase your libido (The Journal of Sexual Medicine, 2009)
- **Cultivate healthy habits** that lead to weight loss (Journal Emotion, 2007)
- **Improve digestion** and lower blood pressure (Harvard Medical School)
- **Decrease your risk of heart attack** (The Stroke Journal, 2009)

- **Help overcome anxiety**, depression, anger and confusion (Psychosomatic Medicine, 2009)
- **Decrease perception of pain** and improve cognitive processing (Wake Forest University School of Medicine, 2010)
- **Increase your focus** and attention (University of Wisconsin-Madison, 2007)
- **Increase the size of your brain**. (Harvard University Gazette, 2006)

If you need more resources on this, the best introduction I have found is a book called **"The Power of Now" by Eckhart Tolle**. Now, there are some new-agey or woo-woo ideas in this book that I don't buy into. I suggest you ignore the things which seem strange, and focus on the mindfulness techniques and exercises, which are excellent. This book alone has changed the lives of so many people. I highly recommend you check it out.

There's another book called "Mindfulness in Plain English" which also gives great step-by-step directions without any new-age stuff in it. You can read both of these books many times and still get fresh insights and wisdom from them.

# Chapter 15
# A Life Of Your Own Design

This is the last chapter. In this chapter I'm going share with you a few last tips that I didn't think fit into any other chapter, but still really shifted the way I think and helped me to overcome my own shyness and social anxiety.

The first thing is

# Treating Yourself Like You Value Yourself

I have found that it is much harder to be confident around people if I don't take steps to show myself that I value myself. For example, if you've sat around your house all day eating Cheetos and playing video games, it's going to be pretty difficult to not think other people are superior to you. It's going to be pretty difficult to feel like you are entitled to other people's friendship and affection when that is the way you are living your life. You are acting in a way that says: "I do not value myself," and that comes across when you talk to other people.

So the first step is to start treating yourself like you value yourself. Think: "If I valued myself, what would I do?" Would you start by taking care of your body? Of course you would. Start exercising and working out, eat healthy food, etc. Once you start doing this, you really do feel entitled to be confident and expressive, because your mind sees that you are taking actions that show you value yourself.

# Having Personal Boundaries

If you let people walk all over you, they will quickly lose respect for you. If you show them you have no boundaries and will let them do whatever they want, then that's exactly what they will do.

**You need to have firm personal boundaries of the types of behaviors you will and will not accept from other people.** This can be small things like making them take their shoes off in your house to showing them you are disappointed when they say they will meet you somewhere and don't.

My favorite example of boundaries happens in everyday conversations. One of the things that shy and socially anxious people don't usually get is that you do not have to respond to everything someone else says! If their comment is lame, you don't have to respond to it. By responding to lame comments, you show them that you don't mind if they don't put in an effort into the conversation. Have a new personal boundary that if someone says something that doesn't really contribute to the conversation, you will not respond to it. This will make the other person realize that they can't just get away with saying something that has no value. They will realize they have to put in an effort if they want to talk to you, and therefore they will value and respect you more.

# Dealing With Family and Old Friends

If you start to change your personality, your family and friends will often do things to sabotage your progress. It's not that they don't want to see you succeed, it's just that most people are scared of changed, and unwilling to accept that you are changing. So what are some obstacles?

## Not being able to act confident around them.

Once you start implementing what you have learnt here, you may start to notice a funny thing happening: you will be able to be confident around new people you meet, but around your family and old friends, you will act more like "the old you." This frustrated me for a long time, until I figured out the reason why.

**I found out that the human brain is set up to create "anchors" for how you act.** This means it remembers how you acted around a person in the past and it pushes you to keep acting that way whenever you are around them now. So while you may be able to be confident and extraverted around a new person you meet, it will be a lot harder to be that way around someone who knows "the old you" well. Unfortunately, there is no quick fix for this. It may take many months to change the way you act around someone you have known for years.

**The best solution I've found is simply to be proactive about meeting new people.** With new people who don't know how you acted in the past, you can form a good impression from the beginning and that colours your whole future relationship together. When I meet people now, they sometimes can't believe it when I tell them I used to have SA.

**You can also try moving to a totally new place** or taking a few months to travel. Going away to college is often the time when some people truly reinvent themselves, because they are free from their past identity and people's past expectations and anchors for how they should act.

**I recently spent six months traveling through Southeast Asia and it was a life-changing experience.** Not just because of the places I visited, but also because I was basically resetting all my old anchors every few days. Every few days, I would take a bus and travel to a new city, with totally new people. It's such an interesting experience to meet so many new interesting people in such a short amount of time. I feel like I got years of social practice in just a few months. You'd be surprised how many people decide to do this type of long-term travel or backpacking, and it can be pretty cheap depending on where you travel. Asia was incredibly inexpensive. I highly recommend doing this at some point in your life.

# They may "test" you.

The second way family and old friends may hold you back if you start trying to act more confident is by "testing" your new confidence. It's almost like they are testing to see if you really are confident and more independent of them now or if you are just putting on an act. How will they test you?

They may try to point out your behaviour and see if you are affected by the attention. They may mention some new clothes you are wearing and see if you appear to be embarrassed. If you try to be more independent they may start telling you to do or not do things just to regain control.

**The key to passing these "tests" is to stay calm.** That's all. Be as calm and relaxed as possible to overcome any feeling of anxiety you may have. The second step is to agree. If they made some observation about your clothes or behaviour that was supposed to embarrass you, simply agree to it. Don't try to defend or justify yourself, just repeat what they said and agree with it. Don't get emotional over it.

For example, "I see you're too good for your family now that you have your new friends," so you can simply respond "Yeah, I have new friends" in the most unemotional and passive voice possible. If they are trying to provoke a reaction from you, they will not get one. Remember, if they can provoke you to react, then they have control over you, which is exactly what they are trying to regain

If you haven't experienced this testing yet and don't know what I'm talking about, then it's probably because you haven't really changed that much yet. This type of testing is really common whenever anyone tries to raise their position in life.

# Conclusion

There isn't much left to be said. If you have read this entire manual, I congratulate you. Most people won't have the determination to get through it all, let alone apply it. Review this book often, keep learning and relearning the principles inside here, and most importantly, DON'T STOP until you have this part of your life handled for good.

Now that you have the intellectual understanding, go out there and get the social experience that will allow you to truly change and cement these skills into yourself. It's gonna take time and patience. Maybe months or even a year or two to reach your desired goals if you are starting out really low.

It sucks that you have this problem in the first place. I know, because I was in your shoes not too long ago. Unfortunately, you cannot control the past. But the good news is, you do have control over what your future will look like.

I'll leave you with this quote:

> "There is nothing for you to go back and live over, or fix, or feel regret about now.
>
> And so - now - knowing all that you know from where you now stand, now what do you want? The answers are now coming forth to you. Go forth in joy, and get on with it."
>
> **- Esther Hicks**

Did you enjoy listening to this system? Are you getting results from what you learned here? If you are, then I would love to hear your story. You can email me at sean@shynesssocialanxiety.com.

Please email me. I'm always glad to receive your comments and feedback. Even if you had some small victory, like going to the grocery store or asking someone out on a date, then feel free to share it with me. Let me know which parts of this system helped you most and which parts can be improved.

Thanks you for taking the time to listen to what I have to say and good luck on your own your journey.

**Until next time,**

**- Sean Cooper**

# Wait! Before You Continue Claim Your FREE Gifts!

Hey, Sean Cooper here.

As a special "Thank You" for buying my book, I'm going to give you these <u>3 free gifts</u> as a surprise bonus:

4. **"How To Always Know What To Say Next" Report** – This report will show you a simple trick to never run out of things to say again. *(Imagine never needing to worry about creating awkward silences or getting a "blank mind"!)*
5. **"Social Circle From Scratch" Report** – This 43 page report will teach you the things you may not have learned while growing up about making friends and getting people to see you as an interesting person.
6. **Weekly email tips and advice** – I'll email you my latest, most cutting-edge techniques and insights into overcoming shyness and social anxiety. *(I promise not to spam you, and you'll be able to unsubscribe from this newsletter any time you want.)*

## To Claim Your Free Gifts, Go Here Now:
## <u>www.ShynessSocialAnxiety.com/freegift/</u>